MEDIEVAL HACKERS

MEDIEVAL HACKERS

Kathleen E. Kennedy

punctum books ✳ brooklyn, ny

MEDIEVAL HACKERS
© Kathleen E. Kennedy, 2015.

http://creativecommons.org/licenses/by-nc-nd/3.0/

This work is Open Access, which means that you are free to copy, distribute, display, and perform the work as long as you clearly attribute the work to the authors, that you do not use this work for commercial gain in any form whatsoever, and that you in no way alter, transform, or build upon the work outside of its normal use in academic scholarship without express permission of the author and the publisher of this volume. For any reuse or distribution, you must make clear to others the license terms of this work.

First published in 2015 by
punctum books
Brooklyn, New York
http://punctumbooks.com

The BABEL Working Group is a collective and desiring-assemblage of scholar-gypsies with no leaders or followers, no top and no bottom, and only a middle. BABEL roams and stalks the ruins of the post-historical university as a multiplicity, a pack, looking for other roaming packs with which to cohabit and build temporary shelters for intellectual vagabonds. We also take in strays.

ISBN-13: 978-0692352465
ISBN-10: 0692352465

Before you start to read this book, take this moment to think about making a donation to punctum books, an independent non-profit press,

@ http://punctumbooks.com/about/

If you're reading the e-book, you can click on the image below to go directly to our donations site. Any amount, no matter the size, is appreciated and will help us to keep our ship of fools afloat. Contributions from dedicated readers will also help us to keep our commons open and to cultivate new work that can't find a welcoming port elsewhere. Our adventure is not possible without your support. Vive la open-access.

Fig. 1. Hieronymus Bosch, *Ship of Fools* (1490-1500)

TABLE OF CONTENTS

1: Medieval Hackers? // 1

2: Hacking Bread Laws // 29

3: The First Hacker Bible // 55

4: Tyndale and the Joye of Piracy // 81

5: Selling Statutes // 117

Homo Hacker? An Epilogue // 139

References // 149

ACKNOWLEDGMENTS

Even small books are the product of legions, and a book this long in the making has many people behind it. I thank Aaron Hawkins: he and my brother were the first Linux users I knew, at a college in a cornfield in the middle 1990s. I wrote the kernel of this book idea on the proverbial bar napkin in front of physicist Bob Klepfer, and the delightfully learned chemist and musician Jon Singer served as a further sounding board. To them and many other scientists and engineers, including Chris Dayton, John Tierney, and Laura Guertin, I offer thanks. You made this book happen.

In front of the backend lies the GUI, and I must thank my network of medievalists and Early Modernists for helping me craft this. The archival research for this book began to take shape on an NEH Summer Seminar organized by John King, James Bracken, and Mark Rankin, and I cannot thank them enough for the opportunity. When I told Brantley Bryant and Karl Steel that I had this book idea, they sent me to Eileen Joy at Punctum, knowing that the people behind an experimental press making use of creative commons licenses would see the potential in my little attempt at media archaeology. Together with my reader Jen Boyle, and punctum's Editorial Associate Paul Megna, who formatted, copy-edited and proofed the book, and the support of many other medievalists, we have all brought you this book. Thank you.

Chapter 1: Medieval Hackers?

Hackers are the last thing most people would associate with the Middle Ages. I copyrighted that sentence as I typed it into my phone while waiting in a grocery line. Indeed, the sentence was copyrighted whether I intended it or not, as under current American law, text is copyrighted the moment it is fixed in media. Such a short description of a textual event hides a wealth of cultural norms, norms which I hope to explore in this book. I am an author. I am the author of that sentence I wrote in the grocery line. However, until I shared that sentence, I had an audience of one, myself. Copyright is fundamentally about who has the right to share a text, that is, who has the right to copy that text, and also who has the right to alter that text. Ultimately, copyright determines who can profit legally from the copying of a text. Historically, however, anyone could copy a text, and profit from that copy. Today if I wish to publish my sentence professionally, as the author I am unlikely to retain the copyright of it. Instead I exchange the copyright with a professional publisher, who then has control over making copies of the sentence I wrote, and over who else can use my sentence. The fact that something else has occurred instead is a tribute to punctum books's interest in openness, commonness, and freedom of information.

As with any cultural practice, copyright has a long history that extends back before there were laws devoted to copyright in the eighteenth century. In the late Middle Ages, authors shared their texts freely. Once completed, a text could be copied by anyone with the skills to do so, and the evidence is overwhelming that this copying included what we today would call "derivative works." That is, copyists felt free to translate texts into other languages, add or subtract material to or from texts, and insert texts into other texts. In every way medieval copyists treated texts as common to all, something we might call "public domain," or, more generally, an "information commons." Occasionally, a king or a clergyman attempted to control this free movement of texts, and then we see people, "medieval hackers," mounting defenses of this information culture. This book will trace intellectual property norms from late medieval England until the crown and a group of printers collaborated successfully to control printing in the 1550s. Despite such channeling, this book considers how the medieval norms of commonness, openness, and freedom of information are still present in our textual culture in the culture of computer hackers. I will also explore how these norms challenge modern copyright law.

The people involved in translating both the Bible and the parliamentary statutes in late medieval England used the very terms of openness and access that hackers use today: they stress commonness, openness, and freedom. This book traces the striking similarity of vocabulary used by contemporary legal theorists and hackers and that of early translators such as the anonymous translators of the Wycliffite Bible, the first complete translation of the Bible into English, later Bible translators such as William Tyndale and George Joye, and early legal translators such as John Rastell. As modern hackers would say, in late medieval England the desire for sacred and secular law in the vernacular was "an itch that had to be scratched," not just for the good of the translators, but for the common good.[1] The major distinction between medieval hackers and modern hackers is that these ideals and the information commons that enabled them were normative in manuscript culture, came to be restricted under the early Tudors, and are now marginal, as are hackers themselves.

It is the rhetoric shared by the medieval information commons and modern hackers that led me to that sentence typed at the grocery store: "hackers are the last thing most people would associate with the Middle Ages." When we think of hackers we think of computers, of programming, maybe even of crime. We are not wrong to think so: today hackers are most frequently computer programmers, and some hackers commit crimes. However many hackers argue that this is a reductive way of thinking about hacking. These hackers counter that hacking is bigger than computer programming. They claim that it is a culture, an ideology. The hacker ideal is a community of equals who gain entrance to the community and position among its hierarchies through skill. This skill is often quite physical, skill at making things, but at a more fundamental and idealistic level it is about having the skill to make something do what the hacker wants it to do, whether or not that thing was designed originally to perform that action. Yet the existence of the notion of "hacker" suggests that this level of skill and control is not the norm today. That we have a word for "hacker" at all suggests that distance, institutional control, or some other physical or cultural barrier prevents manufacture and repurposing from being commonplace.

Such hacking might appear to be strictly limited in time, place, and culture, but I argue instead that hackers are truly medieval, thanks to their relationship with the information commons. Sadly, today many of us think very little about this commons, to which we all have access. The information commons is the "public domain" loosely understood. As we will see in detail later in this chapter the information com-

---

[1] Eric S. Raymond, *The Cathedral and the Bazaar: Musings on Linux*

mons includes all "texts" which the public has the right to circulate and modify as they desire. The information commons does not end with large digital libraries such as Project Gutenberg (www.gutenberg.org), The Internet Archive (archive.org), or Google Books, but extends to a range of computer code, and in the past extended much, much further. We can be pardoned for being unfamiliar with the concept though, as in the early twenty-first century the information commons appears to be shrinking.

Recently institutions and corporations have found it both useful and possible to impose the strictest control in history over the use of information, and this control extends to limiting the information commons. Such wide-ranging control of information is possible thanks to the digital revolution of the late twentieth century. I argue that our modern notion of "the hacker" has developed as this digital control over information has developed. A hacker is an active person, but also a person in opposition, and these inflections are inherent in our uses of the term. The title of this book, *Medieval Hackers,* highlights that opposition with its anachronistic title. The title implies several other aspects of my argument, too. It suggests that the information commons was the norm in medieval England until government and trade institutions and guilds found it both useful and possible to impose controls over the use of information, to limit the information commons. The title implies that these early attempts at information control resulted in the first articulations of hacker culture. This book argues that the historical bedrock on which our own Anglo-American culture is founded is that of an information commons, and that like all bedrock this information commons influences and emerges into culture in various ways today, including in the figure of the hacker.

Media Archaeology

This exploration repurposes a new media theory which itself borrows from the field of geology. Erkki Huhtamo describes "archaeology of the media" as "a way of studying the typical and commonplace in media history—the phenomena that (re)appear and disappear and reappear over and over again and somehow transcend specific historical contexts."[2] Media archaeology offers a more flexible model for considering the past's relationship to the present than Foucauldian genealogy: "media archaeology is first and foremost a methodology, a hermeneutic reading of the 'new' against the grain of the past, rather than a telling of the histories of technologies from past to present."[3] Nevertheless, Lisa Gitelman cautions that in this methodology, the past is too often "represented discretely, formally, in isolation," while the "present retains a highly nuanced or lived periodicity."[4] In short, media archaeology can recover which technologies were new at which periods, but must also fight against seeing this technology in isolation. Clearly media archaeology offers an invigorating way of examining the past, but as with any technique, it must be used cautiously.

In this book, I develop the idea of media archaeology further and extend its use of the geologic analogy. In so doing, my method reads the new against the grain of the past more thoroughly than some others because I employ this method as a medievalist, a twenty-first century scholar at the bottom of the trench, looking up and out at the strata, rather than down and in as do modernists practicing media archaeology. Medievalists develop nuanced pictures of the premodern world and desire to reveal connections between that world and the modern, practices that fight the romanticizing tendency in media archaeology. Medievalists grapple expertly with the difficulties (even impossibilities) inherent in attempting a warts-and-all recreation of ancient culture.

[2] Erkki Huhtamo, "From Kaleidoscomaniac to Cybernerd: Notes Toward an Archeology of Media," *Electronic Culture: Technology and Visual Representation*, ed. Timothy Druckrey (New York: Aperture, 1996), 300 [296–302].

[3] Geert Lovink, *My First Recession: Critical Internet Culture in Transition* (New York: V2 Publishing, 2003), 11.

[4] Lisa Gitelman, *Always Already New: Media, History, and the Data of Culture* (Cambridge, MA: M.I.T. Press, 2006), 11.

One might think of medievalists as rigorously schooled in cultural calculus. Before the seventeenth-century scientist, Isaac Newton discovered how to calculate the area under a curve, astronomers strove mightily using the best mathematical tool at their disposal: trigonometry, which finds the areas of triangles. So the pre-Newtonian astronomers labored to estimate as closely as possible the area under a curve by dividing that curve into thinner and thinner triangles. Eventually they reached a number past which they could no longer figure: we can call this number $.\bar{9}$ (that is, ".9 repeating," or "nines all the way down.") Because $.\bar{9}$ is not a whole number, impossibly tiny portions of the area under the arc remained unmeasured. The magic of calculus was, and remains, truly radical: the scientific community agrees to call that $.\bar{9}$, ONE, to use it as though it is one, because calculations using the fiction of the whole number work. Calculus, the very foundation of modern science and technology, rests on this fiction. Today scientists call this fiction "tolerance," and a particular project's tolerance is based on assessments of that project's margin for error. Historians of all sorts are used to working with "cultural tolerance," and any project which "read[s] the new against the grain of the past" must be especially aware of that margin for error.

When discussing archaeology, the vocabulary of paleontology and geology becomes useful. To practice media archaeology, media theorist Siegfried Zielinski speaks directly of using "certain conceptual premises from paleontology."[5] He expresses clearly the usefulness of the stratigraphic model: "if the interface of my method and the following story are positioned correctly, then the exposed surfaces of my cuts should reveal great diversity, which either has been lost because of the genealogical way of looking at things or was ig-

---

[5] Siegfried Zielinski, *Deep Time of the Media: Toward and Archaeology of Hearing and Seeing by Technical Means*, trans. Gloria Custance (Cambridge, MA: M.I.T. Press, 2006), 7. See also his very wide definition of media, at 33.

nored by this view."[6] For Zielinski, culture accumulates over time as do layers of the earth's crust. Whether for paleontological or archeological purposes, or for oil exploration, modern earth science rests (literally) on the premise of geological stratification. The surface layer, including dirt, plants, dwellings, and mobile phones, is eventually covered, and slowly the surface layer becomes stone due to compression and the chemical exchanges caused by pressure and time. Moreover these stone layers are not static. Strata can be 'lost,' drawn down into the mantle and reheated, and there are other more visible options as well. As the Grand Canyon demonstrates vividly, wind and water can cause erosion, and this can reveal ancient strata. In the form of earthquakes and volcanoes the shifting of the plates making up the earth's crust can uncover hidden strata (and create new strata) quickly and violently.

Of note is how conscious earth scientists are of using "stratigraphy" as a fiction, such as $.\bar{9} = 1$. Strata are made of different types of sediment or volcanic rock, accumulated over time, and strata are identified by the type of rock characteristic of individual strata. Yet strata do not always separate from one another with a thin line, but express relative positions and physical (chemical) compositions. Generally, deeper strata are older than shallower strata (the law of superposition). Individual strata meet at transitional zones, and these can be of great interest to scientists. Like the fiction of 1, stratigraphy allows for a tolerant, two-dimensional representation of four dimensions—the three dimensions of space, and time.

"Cultural stratigraphy" recognizes that our technological landscape of mobile phones rests on top of computers and land-line telephones and telegraphs and letters and messengers going back deep into time. Zielinski's model of media archaeology is quite static, however, as it makes just one cut in motionless strata, and it may not correct for the processes over time that have fossilized deep strata: the medieval mes-

[6] Zielinski, *Deep Time,* 7.

senger we dig up is a pale reflection of the living courier. In a further complication, letters and messengers may be medieval, but they are also modern phenomenon. Even more than geologic strata, cultural strata are shifting and complex. Unlike most modernists, as a medievalist, I am accustomed to working in lower strata and looking up and out to see how younger layers are influenced by older layers in complicated, rather than simple ways. I am practiced at explaining how time has altered a layer from what it once was.[7] That stratigraph of the mobile phone cannot be considered in isolation, but is related also to developments in technology, manufacturing, and globalization of industry and culture.

In this way I am borrowing consciously from the *Annales* school of social history, at the same time as I am informed by the methods of a new generation of scholars. The *annalistes* developed the practice of social history and promoted the use of methods borrowed from the social sciences. One of the fathers of the *annalistes*, Fernand Braudel spends much of the first volume of his magisterial *La Méditerranée* connecting the geology of the Mediterranean basin with its peoples, and I draw from this tradition.[8] Just as the sources I shall rely on throughout this book show topography characteristic of their times and places, they betray also the shifting of strata beneath them. A similar methodology is used to excellent effect by critic Martin Foys in his recent study of the Nunburnholme Cross.[9] In my investigation, translation of texts, additions to them, and methods of copying them reveal stra-

---

[7] Coleman voices concern that hacker ethics are diverse and have changed even inside a few decades: E. Gabriella Coleman, *Coding Freedom: The Ethics and Aesthetics of Hacking* (Princeton: Princeton University Press, 2013), 18. When viewing hacker cultures through history this diversity must be recognized, but I would argue also that looking for commonalities over the long timeline is also worthwhile.
[8] Fernand Braudel, *La Méditerranée et le Monde Méditerranéen*, 2nd edn. (Paris: Librairie Armand Colin, 1966).
[9] Martin Foys, *Virtually Anglo-Saxon: Old Media, New Media, and Early Medieval Studies in the Late Age of Print* (Gainesville: University Press of Florida, 2007).

ta, or layers of accretion, over time. In media archaeological terms, the interaction of hackers with the information commons is today exceptional, but I argue that this same interaction appears to be cultural bedrock underlying, and therefore influencing, all of Anglo-American media culture, at times indirectly, and at times with immediacy.

WHAT IS A HACKER?

The *Oxford English Dictionary* implicitly admits to an untraced origin of the word "hacker." The OED defines "hacker" as "a person with an enthusiasm for programming or using computers as an end in itself," and it lists the first recorded usage in a passage from 1976: "the compulsive programmer, or hacker as he calls himself, is usually a superb technician."[10] Such a description attests to a well-established folk tradition already in place in 1976. (The first recorded instance of "hacker" to refer to illegal programming occurred in the same year.)[11] Yet the word itself is quite old. In fact, the earliest record of the noun "hacker" is medieval: a type of chopping implement was known as a "hacker" from the 1480s.[12] Evidently, over time the term moved from the implement to the person wielding the implement.[13] Today the grammatical slippage remains, as "the hacker hacked the hack" is grammatically sound, if stylistically unfortunate. Notably, even its earliest uses, "hacker" and "hacking" referred to necessary disruption. Arboriculture required careful pruning (with a hacker) to remove unwanted branches and cultivation necessitated the regular breaking up of soil and weeds in between rows of a crop (with a hacker). Such practices broke limbs and turf in order to create beneficial new growth. Such physical hacking resembles the actions of com-

---

[10] "hacker," n. 3a, *Oxford English Dictionary* Online [OED], March 2014, Oxford University Press, http://www.oed.com.
[11] "hacker," n. 3b, OED Online.
[12] "hacker," n. 2a, OED Online.
[13] "hacker," n. 1, OED Online.

puter hackers who claim to identify security exploits (breaking into software) in order to improve computer security, not to weaken it.

As the OED asserts, hackers explore and develop: they make things functional the way they wish them to be. Hacker Eric Raymond distills the definition of "hacker" thusly:

> 1. A person who enjoys exploring the details of programmable systems and how to stretch their capabilities, as opposed to most users, who prefer to learn only the minimum necessary.
>
> 2. One who programs enthusiastically (even obsessively) or who enjoys programming rather than just theorizing about programming...
>
> 6. An expert or enthusiast of any kind.
>
> 7. One who enjoys the intellectual challenge of creatively overcoming or circumventing limitations.
>
> 8. [deprecated] A malicious meddler who tries to discover sensitive information by poking around.... The correct term for this sense is "cracker."[14]

The definition moves from the strictly computer-related to more general ways of experiencing and expressing expertise. It ends with a defense of the legality of hacking: for Raymond criminal hacking is something else, is "cracking," and we will consider this distinction further below. One of the earliest explorers of hacker culture, journalist Steven Levy adds to Raymond's definition and describes what he found in hacker communities in the early 1980s thusly: "it was a philosophy of sharing, openness, decentralization, and getting your hands on machines at any cost to improve the machines and

---

[14] Eric S. Raymond, *The New Hacker's Dictionary*, 3rd edn. (Cambridge, MA: M.I.T. Press, 1996), 234–235.

to improve the world."[15] Hackers such as Richard Stallman and Larry Wall go so far as to describe the decision to be a hacker as a "moral choice" and their rhetoric has been described as evangelical.[16]

Most of the time hackers act within legal bounds, but they can also infringe on proprietary interests (including copyright), sometimes doing so in the name of functionality, and sometimes with larger political goals.[17] Levy explains the thought process behind the actions which hackers sometimes take that run counter to social norms:

> just as information should be clearly and elegantly transported within a computer, and just as software should be freely disseminated, hackers believed people should be allowed access to files or tools which might promote the hacker quest to find out and improve the way the world works.[18]

The recent actions against censorship legislation, in support of file-sharing websites and improved cyber-security by hacker groups such as LulzSec and Anonymous, and of the

---

[15] Steven Levy, *Hackers: Heroes of the Computer Revolution* (New York: O'Reilly Publishing, 2010), ix. (This is an updated twenty-fifth anniversary edition, though unmarked as such in its bibliographic details.)

[16] See Stallman's and Wall's essays in *Open Sources: Voices from the Open Source Revolution,* eds. Chris DiBona, Sam Ockman and Mark Stone (New York: O'Reilly, 1999): Richard Stallman, "The GNU Operating System and the Free Software Movement," 53–70, and Larry Wall, "Diligence, Patience, and Humility," 127–148. Bradley claims Stallman and Raymond have "taken upon themselves to play an evangelical role with regard to [open and free software]": Dale A. Bradley, "The Divergent Anarcho-Utopian Discourses of the Open Soure Software Movement," *Canadian Journal of Communication* 30 (2005): 587 [585–611].

[17] Coleman, *Coding Freedom,* 16. In a sense, exploring the intersection of these activities is the heart of Coleman's recent ethnography of F/OSS hackers, *Coding Freedom*.

[18] Levy, *Hackers,* 95

website WikiLeaks, and even of the leaks by whistle-blower Edward Snowden demonstrate such motivation clearly. Displaying classic hacker culture, the first two of these groups blend a folkloric playfulness with technical expertise and a sense of social justice. Hacking "for the lulz" captures in modern leetspeak (internet chat idiom) the exuberant, frequently dangerous playfulness of trickster figures Coyote or Loki. Though unconfirmed, the recent, reported hacking of computer systems belonging to Iran's Atomic Energy Organization provides a fine example of this enthusiasm and sense of play. Whether hacked by an opposing government, opposition group, or hacktivist organization, the computer systems were deactivated, but also began playing a song by metal band AC/DC at top volume.[19] Recent hacker ethnographer Gabriella Coleman finds humor to be central to hacker culture, as it is deployed to negotiate a culture both egalitarian and at times hierarchical.[20]

Anonymous's use of the Guy Fawkes mask as a symbol of their organization expresses keen awareness of this ancient tradition of hazardous play. The historical Guy Fawkes was what we would today call a religious extremist and a domestic terrorist. Famously, his plot to blow up the Parliament building and kill most of the members of parliament and the royal family was foiled and he was executed. A national holiday, this event is memorialized even today with bonfires, effigies, and masks on 5 November. Anonymous' use of the Fawkes mask hurdles its association with seventeenth-century Catholic domestic terrorism, however, and accepts as its origin Alan Moore's 1980s graphic novel, *V for Vendetta,* and the Wachowskis' translation of that comic to film in 2006.[21]

---

[19] Announced by F-Secure, July 23, 2012, http://www.f-secure.com-weblog/archives/00002403.html (accessed May 18, 2014).
[20] See especially Coleman, *Coding Freedom,* especially Chapter 3.
[21] Both Moore and the Wachowskis gesture toward the historical Fawkes, a rather organic decision for Moore, given the anarchism of his V, but both necessarily and oddly denatured in the Wachowskis' version of the narrative.

In Moore's comic, the Fawkes-mask-wearing main character, V, is a radicalized, violent anarchist, while the Wachowskis' V is a more box office friendly social activist. Anonymous members' use of the mask exploits the space between the two versions of V. While hackers may hack purely in their own interests, larger groups have gained notoriety for their actions on behalf of citizens. Nevertheless, the methods Anonymous and other hacker groups use even in social activism reflect this culture of dangerous play: citizens who find their hacked account information online in plaintext may not feel the "lulz" or the justice. Those aided by Coyote do not always, either.

A hacker himself, Stallman clarifies the distinction between "hacker" and "pirate": "the use of 'hacker' to mean 'security breaker' is a confusion on the part of the mass media. We hackers . . . continue using the word to mean, 'Someone who loves to program and enjoys being clever about it'," or as I myself have heard it generalized: "hackers make things. Bored kids break things."[22] While in modern French, "pirate" is the sole term to express both "pirate" and "hacker," conflating the two obscures the workings of power and property: a pirate steals by definition, while a hacker may not.[23] The annual hacker conventions DEF CON and Black Hat put point on the need for such clarifications. The conventions developed to explore the limitations of computer and network security, and these limitations are demonstrated at presentations during the conventions: attendees must decide on their own how to act on such knowledge. Legal attempts have been made to suppress these demonstrations in the past, but the current trend in DEF CON and Black Hat attendance finds an increasing number of federal and corpo-

---

[22] Stallman, "The GNU Operating System," 53. Much thanks to Jon Singer for the quip. See also entries under "hacker" and "cracker" in Raymond, *Dictionary*, 234, 130.

[23] Laurent Latrive makes a similar remark in discussing cyber- and bio-piracy, and notes that in French, "hacker" is translated as "pirate": Laurent Latrive, *Du bon usage de la piraterie* (Paris: Exils, 2004), 25–26, 115n24.

rate agents attending in an attempt to stay abreast of the information security field.[24]

As early displeasure with DEF CON and Black Hat attests, corporations and government may associate such customary community behavior as sharing with crime and demonize these practices with the criminal term "pirate." Discussing proprietary software development in the early 1980s, Stallman gives this ominous description: "the rule made by the owners of proprietary software was, 'If you share with your neighbor, you are a pirate.'"[25] Yet as Snowden's revelations of pervasive hacking by the NSA and DCHQ remind us even more than the attendance changes at DEF CON, the line between hacking and piracy is both a legal one and highly contested: "the trope of piracy has always been highly mobile, a marker of the very instabilities of those lines that define social and ethical standards."[26] Lawrence Lessig is quick to point out that "neither our tradition nor any tradition has ever banned all 'piracy.'"[27]

---

[24] See for example Kim Zetter, "Feds at DefCon Alarmed after RFIDs Scanned," *Wired*, August 4, 2009, http://www.wired.com/2009/08/fed-rfid/ (accessed May 18, 2014). In 2012, the head of the National Security Administration attended as a speaker: Jim Finkle, "Defcon 2012 Conference: Hackers to Meet with US Spy Agency Chief," *Huffington Post*, July 7, 2012, http://www.huffingtonpost.com/2012/07/20/defcon-2012_n_1691246.html (accessed May 18, 2014). A comparison of the attendance of the two over time can be found at Daniel Nowak, "The Graying of Black Hat, DEFCON, and InfoSec Industry," *TechSource* August 1, 2012, http://www.techsource.ironbow.com/articles/cyber-security/the-graying-of-black-hat-defcon-and-infosec-industry/ (accessed May 18, 2014).

[25] Stallman, "The GNU Operating System," 54. For a meditation on the development of popular understanding of "hacker" and "pirate" as synonymous, see Helen Nissenbaum, "Hackers and the Contested Ontology of Cyberspace," *New Media and Society* 6 (2004): 195–217.

[26] Erin Mackie, "Welcome the Outlaw: Pirates, Maroons, and Caribbean Countercultures," *Cultural Critique* 59 (2005): 29 [24–62].

[27] Lawrence Lessig, *Free Culture: How Big Media Uses Technology and the Law to Lock Down Culture and Control Creativity* (New

As Raymond's definition makes clear, hackers are characterized both by expertise and enthusiasm. The affiliation of the translators we will study in this book with higher education, their enthusiasm for their work, and the importance of communities of translators to them place these translators squarely within a medieval information culture which we today call hacker ideology. Modern or medieval hackers are associated frequently with institutions of higher learning. Levy traces early computer hackers to MIT. John Wyclif and his early followers were all affiliated with the University of Oxford. John Rastell and other early law hackers were trained at the Inns of Court, the legal college of its era. Hacker ethnographer Pekka Himanen recognizes the similarity of hacker culture to academic culture and to medieval work ethics: "openness may be seen as the legacy that hackers have received from the [medieval] university."[28] More than money, hackers are motivated by peer recognition: "for these hackers, recognition within a community that shares their passion is more important and more deeply satisfying than money, just as it is for scholars in academe."[29] A PhD himself, Himanen has worked in and near academia most of his life, and one must recognize the knowing wink in this statement. In the end, neither Anonymous members nor most medieval translators are or were paid for their hacking directly, and so both are motivated by nonmonetary reward.

Some medieval translators were marked with an enthusiasm so zealous that they risked martyrdom for their efforts, and while this may not be identically true of modern hackers, the past few years have seen a string of high-profile arrests. As we shall see in Chapter 4, William Tyndale argued that the Bible was common to all Christians, and that its text should be openly available in English, and free to pass from believer to believer: Tyndale was a hacker. He was tried for his hack-

---

York: Penguin, 2004), 66.
[28] Pekka Himanen, *The Hacker Ethic* (New York: Random House, 2001), 6, 18, 181.
[29] Himanen, *The Hacker Ethic,* 51.

ing, however, and executed for his activities. Even today the hazardous play characteristic of hacker culture can harm the hackers themselves, and not just their targets. New members of the 4chan community can experience all manner of hazing, but the whistle-blowing and attempts to find asylum of Edward Snowden (2013), defection of Sabu from LulzSec (2011), Wikileaks founder Julian Assange's flight from prosecution (2010), and a steady series of arrests of people involved in Anonymous actions (2010-2012) serve as reminders that very real-world consequences remain for hackers who act against the law today.

No less than their medieval counterparts, computer hackers are translators. Analog or digital, translators exercise control over media. Computer code is perpetually translated. Coders translate human languages into computer languages, and then computer language is translated into machine language, the language of zeros and ones in which computers work: one incorrect character and a computer cannot read a program. Levy recounts in detail the great leap forward that occurred as hackers developed more and more robust assemblers (and later compilers) to accomplish these feats of translation, allowing people to program in languages (FORTRAN, BASIC) that were more similar to English than machine language.[30] Like computer hackers, medieval translators were insiders: they had the language skills to open texts, scriptural or legal, into other languages, and thereby make them more accessible.

Computer or human, language is fraught today, and was in medieval England:

> if the languages an individual used—Latin, French, English ... —were in part functions of birth and upbringing, their use in particular domains helped sustain the dynamics of society. Like individual speech acts, moreover, languages had meaning in relation to one another.[31]

---

[30] In a real sense, Levy's entire book revolves around this issue.
[31] Tim William Machan, "French, English, and the Late Medieval

The various computer languages used today by programmers develop and shift in popularity as well, leaving programmers to catch up or miss opportunities. I know a programmer who works as a translator in a quite literal fashion. Effectively he is a computer language translator. He works with databases written in old computer languages and writes patches (and more elaborate programs) that allow these old databases to be read by databases written in newer languages. Hidden from many of us, our contemporary digital culture is saturated with translation, and I go so far as to claim that late medieval England had a culture of translation also. What is surprising is that medieval translators express ideals similar to those of modern-day computer hackers. This startling fact demands that we consider more carefully the medieval antecedents to digital hacking.

COMMON, OPEN, AND FREE: A HACKER'S LIFE FOR ME?

"Commonness, openness, and freedom" is a set of terms that will appear over and over throughout this book, as together those terms form a popular distillation of hacker values.[32] Modern hackers use these terms to describe their goals for the world. Medieval information culture embodied these values. When medieval hackers express their desire for similar values to persist in the face of early attempts to control information, they use the same rhetoric as computer hackers. Each term of the three can be loaded with meaning located in a specific moment in time. For example, John Wyclif's helpers would not have thought of "open" as relating to open

Linguistic Repertoire," *Language and Culture in Medieval Britain: The French of England c. 1100-c. 1500,* ed. Jocelyn Wogan-Browne, with Carolyn Collette, Maryanne Kowaleski, Linne Mooney, Ad Putter and David Trotter (York: University of York Press, 2009), 363 [363–372].

[32] As Coleman makes clear, any such distillation is contested; however, she also admits that statements of hacker ethics do share a "common core" (*Coding Freedom,* 18).

source software as we might today. Yet the base definition remains the same.[33] This section of the chapter will introduce each of these terms.

I am struck by the emphasis computer hackers place on an information commons as necessary to cultural development, since in the Middle Ages manuscript culture was a profound information commons. Medievalists are accustomed to thinking about "commonness." The English law is the "common law." The house of Parliament filled with those below the rank of peer is the House of Commons, and historians and critics have done much work studying the importance of the concept of the common profit to the medieval English.[34] From critic Russell Peck's classic study of the common profit in the medieval poet John Gower's works, to critic Matthew Giancarlo's recent cultural study of the medieval parliament, medievalists have examined the notion of commonness from primarily cultural perspectives, rather than legal ones. Intellectual commons, or "information commons" as I will usually call them, have not been examined. Yet commonness is once again a matter of some debate outside of the field of Medieval Studies, and the terms used are similar to those used by the medieval English when discussing information commons.

The most recognizable and popular voice touting the necessity of a "new commons" is that of cyber-rights activist and Harvard law professor, Lawrence Lessig, and I will use

---

[33] See "common" in the OED Online: adj. and adv. 1, 5, 6, "open," adj., especially 3, 24, 25, 28, and "free," adj., n., and adv., especially 5, 14, 26 and examples the OED does not provide in upcoming chapters.

[34] A *locus classicus* for the study of common profit is Russell Peck, *Kingship and Common Profit in Gower's* Confessio Amantis (Carbondale: Southern Illinois University Press, 1978). For a more recent example of the study of common profit, see Matthew Giancarlo, *Parliament and Literature in Late Medieval England* (Cambridge, UK: Cambridge University Press, 2007) and Kellie Robertson, *The Laborer's Two Bodies: Labor and the "Work" of the Text in Medieval Britain, 1350-1500* (New York: Palgrave, 2006).

his formulation of the issues as a means of outlining the discussion. In *The Future of Ideas: The Fate of the Commons in a Connected World,* Lessig lays out important elements that create a commons. Accordingly a commons is a resource that anyone within the relevant community can use without seeking the permission of anyone else. Such permission may not be required because the resource is not subject to any legal control (it is, in other words, in the public domain). Or it may not be required because permission to use the resource has already been granted.[35] Lessig gives the traditional examples of streets, parks, and texts in the public domain. He also claims that language is a commons, though he does not explore that claim.[36] Lessig's main interest lies in assessing the future of the internet, given that its original design was to be a commons: "open code creates a commons" as Lessig says frequently.[37] Traditionally, commons are maintained in the face of potential for monopolization, and with the understanding that the commons is more valuable if the public has access to it.[38] While custom may not regulate the commons of the internet (or not well), medievalists and Early Modernists can immediately identify the importance of customary prac-

---

[35] Lawrence Lessig, *Code 2.0* (New York: Basic Books, 2006), 198.

[36] Lawrence Lessig, *The Future of Ideas: The Fate of the Commons in a Connected World* (New York: Random House, 2001), 21. In *Code 2.0,* Lessig discusses translation only briefly. He contrasts "translation" or a "strategy [aiming] at finding a current reading of the original Constitution that preserves its original meaning in the present context" with more fundamentalist approaches to the law (160). Indeed, Lessig sees this translation in a linguistic sense: "when dealing with cyberspace, judges are to be translators: Different technologies are the different languages" (165). For Lessig, "a reading of the Constitution that preserves its meaning from one world's technology to another" is a faithful translation, at 166. In short, Lessig would have sense-based cultural translation, not literal word-for-word translation.

[37] Lessig, *Ideas*; see, for example, similar statements on 57, 68.

[38] Lessig, *Ideas*, 87, and Carol Rose, "The Comedy of the Commons: Custom, Commerce, and Inherently Public Property," *University of Chicago Law Review* 53 (1986): 774 [711–781].

tice in the regulation of many sorts of early commons such as pasturing animals.[39] In the following book I argue that in a manuscript culture, texts were part of an information commons. The concept of "the hacker" did not exist, in effect, because everyone was one.

The customary nature of the commons together with the idealism of hacker ideology demonstrate why there is room for a cultural consideration of hackers beyond historian Adrian Johns' masterful *Piracy: The Intellectual Property Wars from Gutenberg to Gates*.[40] Johns views the hacker culture I describe in this chapter as theoretical, rather than actual. Our differences of approach and opinion make good sense, however. In many respects, Johns writes a social history of intellectual property in *Piracy*. Yet there are facets to legal culture which are difficult to see through the lenses of classic legal or social history, as Coleman's ethnography aptly illustrates. Custom is one example. Further, ideals can be powerful without always extending to practice, and the idealistic expressions of hackers about their culture, whether in the twenty-first century or sixteenth century, can influence culture whether or not they are practiced as preached. This study explores the same history of hacking Johns traces, but does so for long before his research begins and employs a more cultural method.

This recent consideration of commonness, the "work not of economists but of lawyers and legal theorists" fits into discussion of intellectual property by political philosophers Michael Hardt and Antonio Negri in their philosophical opus on the commons, *Commonwealth*.[41] Hardt and Negri develop

---

[39] Rose is particularly emphatic that custom may prevent a "tragedy of the commons" where commons are over-used to the point that they are destroyed; see Rose, "The Comedy of the Commons," 739–749. For a pop culture overview of the tragedy of the commons, see Ryan North, *Dinosaur Comics* 1731, June 10, 2010, http://www.qwantzp.com/index.php?comic=1731 (accessed May 18, 2014).

[40] Adrian Johns, *Piracy: Intellectual Property Wars from Gutenberg to Gates* (Chicago: University of Chicago Press, 2009).

[41] Michael Hardt and Antonio Negri, *Commonwealth* (Cambridge,

a political philosophy based on the commons as neither public nor private. While we can easily see how the commons and private property can be in tension, they remind us also that "it is important to keep conceptually separate the common—such as common knowledge and culture—and the public, institutional arrangements that attempt to regulate access to it."[42] These scholars emphasize the social character of the commons, that it is not only air and water, but also language and social networks.[43] Those social networks are fundamental to hacker culture and medieval information culture alike.

The historical possibilities latent in the notion of an information commons are sketched out strikingly by political scientist Steven Weber: "people take the religious 'code,' modify it, recombine it with pieces of code from elsewhere, and use the resulting product to scratch their spiritual itch."[44] As we will see in Chapters 3 and 4, the Bible already existed when the fourteenth-century Wycliffite translators and the sixteenth-century Lutheran translators approached it. In translating it, they modified the Bible by "recombining" it with other languages, or "pieces of code from elsewhere," and they used the resulting vernacular Bible to "scratch their spiritual itch" for scripture in English. A similar equation applies to the translation of the law. Neither the Wycliffites nor the Tudor translators could have accomplished their task (or conceived of it in the same way) had the Bible not been part of a traditional information commons.

Nevertheless, a central thread throughout this book is that institutions attempted at various times in late medieval England to control or gate the information commons, to render at least parts of it proprietary. In Chapter 3, I discuss

---

MA: Belknap Press, 2009), 281.

[42] Hardt and Negri, *Commonwealth,* 282.

[43] See for example Hardt and Negri, *Commonwealth,* 171, and for their "two notions of the common," viii, 139.

[44] Steven Weber, *The Success of Open Source* (Cambridge, MA: Harvard University Press, 2004), 229.

Archbishop Thomas Arundel's laws outlawing the spread of the new English Bible (1407-1409). Chapter 4 recounts the struggle of hackers against the laws of Henry VIII's administration (1509-1547) that tried to curtail the hackers' new Bible translations. In a sense, Arundel and Henry VIII attempted to exert proprietary control over the Bible's text and claimed a legal right to identify who would be allowed to copy the Bible or translate it into English. Today, translation is considered to produce a derivative work, and derivatives are protected under current copyright law. At the end of Chapter 5, we will see how a group of law printers convinced Mary I (1553-1558) to agree to incorporate and grant them the right to regulate all printing, institutionalizing a level of proprietary interest never before accomplished.

Closing a commons restricts other aspects of society in ways that could not have been completely apparent to the sixteenth-century printers, but are readily evident today. Without linking their use of these terms to hacker culture, Hardt and Negri make it clear that a society based on the commons requires openness.[45] Indeed, in the worldview proposed by the pair, capital itself is "understood not simply as social relation but as an *open* social relation" (emphasis original).[46] Furthermore, Hardt and Negri's formulation implies free circulation. Both openness and freedom are recognized by modern hackers as integral parts of their ideology.

Built on the hacker tradition of an information commons, the open source software model advocated by Stallman, Himanen, and other hackers highlights the second ideal of hacker culture: openness. From operating systems (Linux) to web browsers (Firefox), these programs are "open" to all. Any user can see the code and work to improve it if she or he so desires. Access to open source code is assured through a range of licenses (like the copyright on this book) designed to

---

[45] See Hardt and Negri, *Commonwealth,* 308, where the openness is a radical one, where communication networks are open and accessible and code is open, a veritable restatement of hacker ideals.
[46] Hardt and Negri, *Commonwealth,* 150.

perpetuate the openness of these programs, and most of these programs are available to users gratis. In this way open source culture can be free in multiple senses.[47]

Openness can be seen in other arenas of information culture as well. Today we own many electronics that exist in boxes, but we cannot open those boxes ourselves because something has broken and we want to fix it, or even just because we want to see inside. These boxes are closed on many levels. In contrast, building a piece of electronics out of parts (something that is still possible) may be far more labor intensive than cutting open a packing box, or removing the cover from a desktop computer, but once assembled, any part can be replaced, and parts can be added over time to keep the system up to date. That is an open box. The analogy works also in fields far from electronics. Although your Great Aunt Biddy may never divulge her recipe for barbecue, you can walk into a grocery store and buy each ingredient and make your own and sell it at a block party: cooking from scratch is an open process. Openness can be found in parts of the modern publishing field, too. Rather than a standard copyright, the present book is protected by a Creative Commons Attribution-Noncommercial-NoDerivs 3.0 Unported License.[48] This frees a reader to share this book as long as it is attributed to me and the reader does not make any money in so sharing this book. However, this license does not render this book entirely open, as the "No Derivatives" clause prohibits building on this book, or even translating it without permission. A related prohibition, "do not fork code" (do not create a separate project using someone else's code without permis-

---

[47] The history, even ethnography, of this paragraph is repeated in many places. See for example, *Open Sources 2.0*, eds. DiBona, Cooper and Stone; and also see Lessig's and Himanen's works already cited. See also Weber, *Success,* 228. Coleman's ethnography stresses the legal training that the development of open source software has encouraged among the hacking communities.

[48] See the description here for further details: http://creative-commons.org/licenses/by-nc-nd/3.0/.

sion) is a modern hacker custom that we will also see at work in early sixteenth-century England in Chapter 4.

There is a growing understanding that openness has been prioritized at previous points in history. Raymond characterizes the distinctions between industry software development and open source development as "the cathedral and the bazaar," explicitly linking industry hierarchies with the medieval Church (and hackers with a globalized, exoticized marketplace).[49] Programmer Tim O'Reilly sees open source as having a history, too: "instead of thinking of open source only as a set of . . . software development practices, we do better to think of it as a field of scientific and economic inquiry, one with many historical precedents, and part of a broader social and economic story."[50] Consultant Eugene Kim sees "culture[s] of openness" occurring repeatedly through time and emphasizes the necessity of effective communication in creating these cultures, effective communication which "begins with shared language."[51]

The third hacker ideal is freedom, and this can have multiple resonances. Of course, free can refer to gratis, costing nothing. More often, however, freedom is associated with access and circulation: code circulates freely, easily, among users. According to hackers copyright is the opposite of freedom. Copyright, even the prehistory of copyright, is a product of the narrowed cultural options that critic James Simpson and I argue emerge in the 1540s. The scholarship concerning early copyright and the prehistory of copyright, the Stationers' Company, Tudor printing monopolies, and Elizabethan plagiarism is deep and probing, but it is entirely for-

---

[49] Raymond, *Bazaar*, 27–78. I have seen no discussion of the implications of Raymond's choice of "bazaar," so redolent of colonialism, to contrast with "cathedral." Raymond's use of "bazaar" as an active resistance against "the cathedral" begs for postcolonial critique.

[50] Tim O'Reilly, "The Open Source Paradigm Shift," in *Open Sources 2.0*, eds. DiBona, Cooper and Stone, 271 [253–272].

[51] Eugene Kim, "Everything is Known," in *Open Sources 2.0*, eds. DiBona, Cooper and Stone, 297, 303, 304 [297–306].

ward-looking.[52] None of these scholarly works gives more than a cursory backward glance into the Middle Ages to find cultural precedent. At the end of Chapters 4 and 5, I gesture toward this closure of options characteristic of the 1540s, but the meat of this book lies in describing the culture that precedes this closed notion of intellectual property, and against which, in the end, institutional control successfully thrust.

MAKING MEDIEVAL HACKERS

To unpack the idea of an information commons as the bedrock of modern information culture this book explores the similarities between medieval English manuscript culture and modern computer hacker culture. First, the way medieval translators worked with text is very similar to what computer hackers do with code: they assess, modify and disseminate it. For modern hackers, modification can be structural, changing how code does its job, or linguistic, translating the language in which the code is written. For medieval translators, modification can also be structural, paraphrasing the psalms, for example, or linguistic, translating a statute into English. Hackers produce code, and in order to explore the medieval stratum of this practice one must examine texts and their production. While the information commons held across medieval Europe, I concentrate on medieval England as the foundation of modern Anglo-American law. Within

---

[52] Just a few of the many possible examples are essays in the recent *Privilege and Property: Essays on the History of Copyright*, eds. Ronan Deazley, Martin Kretschmer and Lionel Bently (London: OpenBook Publishers, 2010); Jody Greene, *The Trouble with Ownership: Literary Property and Authorial Liability in England, 1660-1730* (Philadelphia: University of Pennsylvania Press, 2005); Joseph Loewenstein, *The Author's Due: Printing and the Prehistory of Copyright* (Chicago: University of Chicago Press, 2002); Mark Rose, *Authors and Owners: The Invention of Copyright* (Cambridge, MA: Harvard University Press, 1993); and Debora Shuger, *Censorship and Cultural Sensibility: The Regulation of Language in Tudor-Stuart England* (Philadelphia: University of Pennsylvania Press, 2006).

medieval English culture, I draw my examples from the two most frequently copied texts, the Bible and the parliamentary statutes.

Approached from a practical standpoint, both the Bible and the statutes are similar to computer code today. As technologies, computers, the Bible, and the statutes require similar apparatus: all are sites of massive information storage and require refined techniques for information retrieval. Translation issues among computers, the Bible, and the statutes are similar as well. In a computer program, a single punctum out of place renders the code unreadable, and the program unusable. The discussion of whether to translate word-for-word or for sense is as old as Bible translation itself, but rarely do scholars consider translating the statutes in the same light. As in programming, the very wording of the Bible and the statutes was powerful, whether that power emanated from God or from the king and parliament, and therefore translation gave rise to similar methodological problems in each.

Yet medieval hackers were never called "hackers" at all because they were normative in a way computer hackers have never been. Only at times when the information commons is under threat do both groups employ the same rhetoric when explaining the importance of text and their roles in manipulating it. As manuscript culture gave way to print culture, ways of thinking about the possibility of text, of dissemination, of authorship, of ownership over information changed. At times these shifts were perceived as threatening the information commons, and then medieval hackers spoke out self-consciously. A similar paradigm-shift occurred in the late twentieth century, with the rise of digital technologies and the internet. Attempts to shut down file-sharing service The Pirate Bay led to the development of political "Pirate Parties" in several countries. Anonymous has also been involved in actions against corporations or governments that they view as threats to the free movement of information. We are today familiar with the reactions of at least parts of the hacker community to these perceived threats.

Simpson calls the type of information culture we shall see

throughout this book, that I call an information commons, a "plausible alternative modernity."[53] Indeed it is plausible: computer hackers support this very culture today. We will discuss "differing definitions of self and communities," of a "communitarian tradition," but it will be one of translation, of manipulation of texts, not of reading alone, as Simpson explores.[54] Once these medieval traditions had been firmly overcome, Simpson paints a bleak image of the 1540s, and we might well wonder how bright our own future is in a world increasingly cordoned from Hardt and Negri's common and its flourishing, nourishing social networks.[55]

This book does not tell a triumphalist narrative of "the hacker." Hacker culture used to be normative, but in the early age of print, in the 1540s, various cultural forces worked together to gate this vigorous textual culture and change it radically. To control access to texts and textual manipulation was revolutionary then. Today it is normative, and instead, arguing for open access to texts and the right to manipulate them is considered revolutionary (or simply criminal). Moreover, the technologies we have today allow for unprecedented control over texts and their manipulation. The medieval hackers "lost": their culture was overwhelmed by a new way of life. Today, we must look back carefully at this moment that gave birth to our own information culture and use that examination to inform our decision to be spectators or agents in the current battles over access to information.

---

[53] Simpson, *Burning to Read: English Fundamentalism and Its Reformation Opponents* (Cambridge, MA: Belknap Press, 2010), 3.
[54] Simpson, *Burning to Read*, 32–33.
[55] Simpson, *Burning to Read*, 155.

Chapter 2: Hacking Bread Laws

The "Renew, Reuse, Recycle" motto of late twentieth- and twenty-first-century America had an early twentieth-century echo from the Great Depression and World War II: "use it up, wear it out, make it do, or do without." Both phrases express the importance of making things as useful as possible for as long as possible, and the earlier expression recognizes that a failure of sustainability leaves us bereft. For hackers, sustainability is a passion. In an era of disposable electronics, hackers are keen to extend the functioning lives of machines by repairing them or reprogramming them. As we saw in Chapter 1, hackers may expend this effort out of selfishness, out of simple joy in hacking, but may also act for the common good. To accomplish this, however, hackers must truly own the "boxes" they modify; this is a current point of contention between hackers and electronics manufacturers. Even the first iPad had no way for an owner to access the battery (without a sledgehammer). Tablet and iPad screens tend to be fused to the motherboard, prohibiting any significant repair and requiring replacement of most of the unit, rather than replacing individual parts. Likewise most software cannot be customized, developed, or even fixed except by specialists licensed by the software company. Such single-purposefulness and limitation of code, of text, frustrates modern hackers, and would not even have been possible in medieval manuscript culture.

This chapter establishes the information commons as a deep stratum of our present culture. As such, the medieval information commons affects our modern world both indirectly through intervening cultural layers, and directly, in those narrow places where the information commons persists. Texts in medieval England were common to the point of promiscuity. Anyone with the skill to write could copy any text. Further, anyone could modify that text by adding or subtracting, developing, or translating the text into another language. Examples of such hacking in literary texts are legion. The elaborate revision history (some authorial and some not) of the long poem *Piers Plowman* is an extreme example.[1] However, we might think too how the monk and poet John Lydgate "completed" Geoffrey Chaucer's *Canterbury Tales* with additional material. As we will see in Chapter 3, another cleric, Richard Maidstone, translated and paraphrased the Penitential Psalms, and this paraphrase was selected by a patron or copyist to replace the Latin Penitential Psalms in an otherwise Latin prayer-book.[2] There is no reason to suspect that the people making and reading these works of literature were hackers self-consciously: their products championed commonness, openness, and freedom only because their textual culture promoted these ideals generally. The iPad's inflexibility was simply not conceivable in such a culture.

Today literature is heavily copyrighted, but it was manifestly part of the information commons in the Middle Ages and is therefore unsuitable to use as a control group. For my

---

[1] See the extraordinary book by Lawrence Warner, *The Lost History of* Piers Plowman: *The Earliest Transmission of Langland's Work* (Philadelphia: University of Pennsylvania Press, 2011).
[2] New York, Morgan Library, MS M. 99.

purposes, I had to investigate a form of text that could conceivably have been controlled in order to establish that what we today call the information commons existed in late medieval England and was the normal state of affairs. Instead of literary examples, therefore, I chose statute law as my example because it was as controlled as the Middle Ages could manage. If the powerful in medieval England could control a text, the texts of the law would seem to be where they would concentrate that ability. If examination shows that law texts do not remain controlled, if they acquire layers of accretion and shift and bend according to copyists' desires, then either institutional control was ineffective, or there was no real effort at control at all, and texts were universally part of an information commons. (Remember that just as a commons is guided by custom, so an information commons does not suggest a free-for-all.) As we do today, the medieval English had a legal system based both on written law, statutes agreed upon in parliament, and on precedent law, determined in the courts.

Unlike literature, medieval English law was as close to monolithic and proprietary as could exist at the time. As law, the authoritative text of the statutes was not supposed to vary. In order to preserve that fixity, statute law existed in the learned languages of Latin and a special dialect of French, called "law French." In England, the text of laws had to be carefully and correctly stated whenever it was used: precise wording mattered. To establish that precise wording, the only official copy of the statutes was the Statute Roll kept at the Exchequer, and not a single copy elsewhere had formal legal validity.[3] When copies were made, we even have evidence of them being checked for accuracy against the Statute Roll.[4]

---

[3] Don C. Skemer emphasizes the unofficial nature of any copy of the statutes in "From Archives to the Book Trade: Private Statute Rolls in England, 1285-1307," *Journal of the Society of Archivists* 16 (1995): 194 [193–206]. See also H.G. Richardson and George Sayles, "The Early Statutes," *Law Quarterly Review* 50 (1934): 544, 548 [201–223, 540–571].

[4] Skemer, "Book Trade," 199.

Despite all this cultural regulation, however, evidence abounds that the statutes were part of an information commons. In fact, the ad hoc modification of statutes supports in a striking and surprising fashion Hardt and Negri's caution that the common is not public, as it is distinct from the regulations directing the use of a common. Despite their unofficial status (once duplicated), statutes were copied in legion: nearly 500 copies of statute collections remain from medieval England.[5] Only a tiny minority of these copies was formally checked against the Statute Roll for accuracy. Statutes were also modified and developed in various ways. They were translated into English, the common tongue, but not a language used much in formal legal practice until later in the fifteenth century. Remarkably, statutes in English were even edited: local law and custom was sometimes threaded through national law in "quilted" legal anthologies.

Law translators are analogous to modern computer programmers. The law translators we study in this chapter and Chapter 5 had access to the languages necessary for translation, just as modern computer hackers have access to the "learned" computer languages. Also, law translators had access to exemplars of the texts to be translated just as computer hackers rarely build code from scratch, but begin with an exemplar, which they modify. Both law translators and computer hackers move easily inside the information commons. Both work to make texts useful.

Perhaps the most-used statute in medieval England was the Assize of Bread, and derivatives of this statute form the

---

[5] For various counts of statute collections, see Skemer "Book Trade," 201n16; Don C. Skemer, "Sir William Breton's Book: Production of *Statuta Angliae* in the Late Thirteenth Century," *English Manuscript Studies 1100-1700*, eds. Peter Beal and Jeremy Griffiths (London: British Library, 1997), 24 [24–51]; and Don C. Skemer, "Reading the Law: Statute Books and the Private Transmission of Knowledge in Late Medieval England," in *Learning the Law: Teaching and the Transmission of Law in England, 1150-1900*, eds. Jonathan A. Bush and Alain Wijffels (London: British Library, 1999), 115–131 (and note the correction to these numbers, at 115).

concentration of this chapter. Few people in medieval England baked their own bread: bread ovens were costly to heat, and so in country, town, and city, people brought their loaves to a communal oven to be baked, or purchased bread directly from professional bakers running those ovens.[6] Bread was such a staple foodstuff that its cost was regulated from a very early date at the national and local levels. Dated traditionally to 1256, the Assize of Bread probably fixed in writing customary practices that were much older. The Assize was used to regulate the prices and profits involved with selling bread, and was "one of the most widely enforced statutes in medieval England."[7] Officials assayed bakers' loaves regularly and the Assize of Bread was more thoroughly developed than the related Assize of Ale, and apparently more consistently policed, an impression that the manuscript record bears out.[8] The goal of the Assize of Bread was that a specified loaf would be sold at a constant price, but the weight of that loaf would vary based on the cost of grain.[9] Together with tables of weights and prices, the Assize outlined acceptable profits due to the bakers. This range of information challenged medieval copyists and translators, and this chapter explores the various solutions they developed to render this body of in-

---

[6] This paragraph is based on discussion in the following: James Davis, "Baking for the Common Good: a Reassessment of the Assize of Bread in Medieval England," *Economic History Review* 57 (2004): 465–502, and Claire Fennell, "The Assize of Bread (1256)," in *Beowulf and Beyond,* eds. Hans Sauer and Renate Bauer (Frankfurt am Main: Peter Lang, 2007), 183–196. For bread laws in London specifically, see Gwen Seabourne, "Assize Matters: Regulation of the Price of Bread in Medieval London," *The Journal of Legal History* 27 (2006): 29–52. Though primarily concerned with the second half of the twin assize, see also Judith Bennett, *Ale, Beer, and Brewsters in England: Women's Work in a Changing World, 1300-1600* (Oxford: Oxford University Press, 1996).
[7] Davis, "Baking for the Common Good," 466. For dating, see Fennell, "Assize," 184.
[8] Davis, "Baking for the Common Good," 466n109.
[9] Davis, "Baking for the Common Good," 466.

formation useful to their audiences.

The rest of the chapter will proceed in three sections. First, I will introduce the shift in language used in law in late medieval England generally. As we saw in Chapter 1, Lessig claims language to be a commons, but surely this is less true of learned languages than the common tongue. Translation is a fundamental kind of textual transformation and produces a derivative text, and such derivatives are normal in an information commons. Additionally, we might think of such derivatives as an additional layer of accretion, sedimented atop the original text. On a wiki such as Wikipedia, one can view all the changes made to a page, and with those revisions in mind the page at any moment in time becomes many-layered. Translation counts as a significant type of revision. Then, I will consider a second type of accretion, textual derivatives. These examples are translations, but they add various kinds of material to the statute text. Finally, I will consider a third kind of accretion, textual derivatives, which alter the form of the statutes themselves. Texts could be laid out in various formats on the page, and in a range of types of volume. For medieval or modern hackers, the proof of success is functionality, utility.[10] The range and skill displayed in each of these layers added to the Assize of Bread suggests that for all its counter-intuitiveness, statute law was part of the information commons, and useful textual products were sustainable and could endure in the marketplace for a very long time indeed.

USE IT UP: FRENCH AND LATIN AS LEGAL LANGUAGES

While a state with laws preserved in learned languages seems

---

[10] This generalization began in the hacker community, and is implicit in Raymond's stipulation that the quality of a released (nonbeta) program is determined by how well it works. See Eric S. Raymond, *The Cathedral and the Bazaar: Musings on Linux and Open Source by an Accidental Revolutionary* (New York: O'Reilly, 1999), 115.

impossibly Byzantine today, the complexities of "law English" that have come to replace the specialized Latin and French dialects might appear on closer examination to give cold comfort, as anyone who has labored to read through any Terms of Service knows. Of course, maintaining the law in languages other than the common tongue can be considered a form of control over the law. However, for much of medieval English history, this control was not particularly institutionally directed and derived organically from the languages used in education, Latin and French, rather than artificially, from legislation. Nevertheless, the variety of languages of medieval English law bears on our thinking about law translation as an example of the information commons at work.

Long after the Norman Conquest rendered French and Latin the languages of government and law in England, English began to be discussed formally as a potential legal language beginning in 1362, with the Statute of Pleading, the first law concerning legal language in English history.[11] While everyone in late medieval England had a good chance of being exposed to English, French, and Latin regularly, levels of comprehension and fluency could vary enormously.[12] A law

---

[11] The Statute of Pleading has been traditionally, and mistakenly, discussed as a linguistic turning point. See Mark Ormrod's corrective in "The Use of English: Language, Law, and Political Culture in Fourteenth-Century England," *Speculum* 78 (2003): 752 [750–787]. For well-known uses of this trope, see V.J. Scattergood, *Politics and Poetry in the Fifteenth Century* (New York: Barnes and Noble, 1972), 13, and Albert C. Baugh and Thomas Cable, *A History of the English Language*, 5th edn. (Upper Saddle River, NJ: Prentice Hall, 2002), 149–150. For a longer bibliography, see Ormrod, "The Use of English," 750n2.

[12] The foundation for discussions of kinds of literacy and languages of literacy in medieval England is M.T. Clanchy's *From Memory to Written Record: England 1066-1307*, 2nd edn. (Oxford: Oxford University Press, 1993). In addition, important interventions have been made in exploring auralities as levels of literacy as well, most notably by Joyce Coleman in *Public Reading and the Reading Public in Late Medieval England and France* (Cambridge, UK: Cambridge University Press, 1996). For the most recent interventions in the

concerning legal language falls into Hardt and Negri's "public" category: it seeks to regulate the use of the common, of the language itself. In the Statute of Pleading, however, the regulation was to increase use of the common (in whatever limited a fashion), rather than restrict it. This is the one example I have found of hacker rhetoric that did not occur at a time when the medieval information commons was threatened with restrictive regulation. Given that information commons function inside custom, however, any legislative (public) regulation might be productive of a statement of hacker values, whether that legislation was restrictive or not.

Though the Statute of Pleading was no great leap forward for English, nevertheless it expresses rhetoric of linguistic access that we will see used by hackers throughout this book, and it sounds a number of complaints with the legal system which we shall see reinvoked in the early sixteenth century:

> great misfortunes have befallen many of the realm because the laws, customs, and statutes of the said realm are not commonly known in the same realm, since they are pleaded, counted, and judged in the French language, which is very much unknown in the said realm, so that the people who plead or are impleaded ... have no understanding or knowledge of what is said for them or against them by their [lawyers].[13]

A corollary was that if courtroom dialogue was in English, "the said laws and customs would be learned and known and better understood in the language used in the said realm, so that every man of the said realm might better organize his

---

area of French fluency in England, see the essays in Jocelyn Wogan-Browne, ed., with Carolyn Collette, Maryanne Kowaleski, Linne Mooney, Ad Putter and David Trotter, *Language and Culture in England: The French of England, c. 1100-1500* (York: York Medieval Press, 2009).

[13] I use Ormrod's translation here. Compare *Statutes of the Realm*, 11 vols. (London, 1810-1825), I:375 (hereafter SoR) to Ormrod, "The Use of English," 756.

affairs without offending the law."[14]

While only commonness is invoked in the Statute of Pleading explicitly, openness is also implied. The statute law was common to all and was supposed to be common knowledge: the implication is that it should be open, accessible, to all. If the law was not open, this put the common people at risk, and ran afoul of the Magna Carta's provisions against unjust punishment and imprisonment, and for regular legal procedures. Law that is not practiced "commonly" leads to "great misfortunes." One of the translators we will discuss in Chapter 5 used similar language and saw the Statute of Pleading as a step in the right direction.

In 1362, neither parliament nor the king was arguing for a legal information commons, as the document itself makes clear. The statute is recorded in law French, and ends with the king demanding that, while courtroom procedure was to take place in "in the Tongue of the Country," law was to be recorded in Latin.[15] So much for an open, common law—the statute shows no interest in making English law more transparent for the common people at large, but simply for a slightly larger group than previously. Notably absent from this statute is any explicit rhetoric about the common good, an additional line of argument employed by legal translators in the sixteenth century, as we will see in Chapter 5.

Yet, following the custom of an information commons, the common tongue made inroads into the law, like one layer of sediment gradually covering another. The greatest shift toward English use in the law occurred in the fifteenth century, and most of the "hacked" statutes discussed in this chapter date to that century. Evidence exists that beginning in the

---

[14] Likewise, for this section, I have quoted Ormrod's superior translation. Compare Ormrod, "The Use of English," 756 to SoR, I:375.

[15] SoR, I:376. For discussion of languages of written and spoken law before 1362, see George Woodbine, "The Languages of English Law," *Speculum* 18 (1943): 395–436, and Paul Brand's more recent corrections in "The Languages of the Law in Later Medieval England," in *Multilingualism in Later Medieval Britain*, ed. D.A. Trotter (Cambridge, UK: D.S. Brewer, 2000), 63–76.

1362 parliament, English was used increasingly by the House of Commons, as well as in the assembled Parliament, containing the Commons and the House of Lords.[16] Personal communications of the King began to appear in English under Henry V (1413-1422).[17] The office of the Privy Seal switched to using English after the 1420s.[18] The parliament rolls began to be kept regularly in English after 1450.[19] The court of Chancery recorded appeals in English consistently beginning in the reign of Henry VI too (1422-1461, 1470-1471).[20] The text of royal proclamations was composed in English beginning in Edward IV's reign (1461-1470, 1471-1483).[21] As we will see in Chapter 5 statutes began to be printed in English under Henry VII (1485-1509). However, the transition to English law was not complete for centuries (sedimentation can take a long time). The Chancery did not issue anything under the great seal in English in the fifteenth century at all, and the great financial arm of government, the Exchequer continued to use Latin in its instruments until the nineteenth century.[22] While Latin and French were not entirely "used up" in this period, the fifteenth century marked a growing acceptance of written English, an acceptance echoed in the manuscript record of English translations of the statutes.

---

[16] Ormrod, "The Use of English," 777–780. For Parliament's move to use English, see also John Fisher, "Chancery and the Emergence of Standard Written English in the Fifteenth Century," *Speculum* 52 (1977): 880n37 [870–899].
[17] Ormrod, "The Use of English," 785.
[18] Ormrod, "The Use of English," 785. Elna-Jean Young Bentley, *The Formulary of Thomas Hoccleve*, Ph.D. diss., Emory University, 1965, shows that Privy Seal use in the 1420s remained in the learned languages.
[19] Fisher, "Chancery," 880. Fisher's main concentration, Chancery, records its judicial decisions systematically in English from the beginning of Henry VI's reign (Fisher, "Chancery," 888).
[20] Fisher, "Chancery," 888.
[21] Ormrod, "The Use of English," 786.
[22] Ormrod, "The Use of English," 785. See also Fisher, "Chancery," 877.

Make It Do: The Texts of the Assize of Bread and the Statute of Winchester

Unless they wished to "do without," people "made do" by transforming the statutes in significant ways, and adding layers of textual accretion. In all of the cases we will examine below the statutes have been altered from the official version to greater or lesser degrees, demonstrating that users felt free to modify these legal texts to suit their own local conditions. These transformations are striking when we consider the fixity usually ascribed to the text of laws.

In the modern record of the Old Statutes, the Assize of Bread uses the following terms:

> When a quarter of wheat is sold for 12 pence then wastel bread of a farthing shall weigh 6 pounds and 16 shillings. But bread cocket of the same grain and fineness of flour shall weigh more than wastel by 2 shillings. And cocket bread made of lower price grain shall weigh more than wastel by 5 shillings. Bread made into simnel shall weigh 2 shillings less than wastel. Bread made of whole wheat shall weigh a cocket and a half. Bread of treet (bran) shall weigh 2 wastels. And bread of wheat shall weigh two great cockets. When a quarter of wheat is sold for 18 pence then wastel bread of a farthing white and well baked shall weigh 4 pounds, 10 shillings, 8 pence. [continued list of prices] And it is to be known, that in every quarter of wheat, as it is proved by the King's Bakers, a baker may gain 4 pence, and the bran, and two loaves in profit. For the three servants, 1 pence, a halfpenny for two lads, the same for salt, for kneading, for candles, 2 pence for wood and a halfpenny for the sifting.[23]

Today this reads slowly, if we can make our way through it at

---

[23] The language of this Assize has been modernized. For the early nineteenth-century English version, and the Latin on which it was based, see SoR, I:199–200.

all. Part of the confusion is the mixture of unfamiliar volumetric measures with weights and prices. Overall, as the price of a measure of grain, called a quarter of wheat, rose, the size of a loaf made from flour derived from that quarter of wheat was supposed to decrease so that the price of it remained the same. Bran bread was heavy and dismissed as the poorest quality. The finest, lightest flour produced the purest white bread. In this way, in theory, people could always afford to purchase bread, though a lesser quality or quantity when grain prices were high. At the same time, the profits due to the baker were spelled out carefully, not only how much profit he was to take, but also the business expenses that profit covered.

Given how necessary it was on a regular basis, the Assize of Bread is one of the most common laws to be found in English translation.[24] Since its goal was protection for both consumer and producer, it is no surprise to find it revised to suit local conditions: as James Davis points out, "overall the implementation of [the Assize of Bread] in the localities was a vibrant example of how central initiatives could be successfully adapted and interpreted through local courts and officials."[25] In laws like this one, vocabulary plays an important role: specific types of bread made of specific types of flour and baked in certain ways must be identifiable to the statute's audiences.[26] While there was certainly overarching similarity in bread names across medieval England, any official had to

---

[24] Aside from one complete translated collection which includes the Assize, Oxford Bodleian, MS Rawlinson B. 520, I have found eleven manuscripts contain the translated Assize of Bread and Ale in whole or in part: Oxford, Bodleian Library, MSS Douce 16, Douce Charters 62 (also known as Douce Charters a. 1. f. 9), Tanner 407, Rawlinson D. 939; Oxford, Balliol College, MS 354; London, British Library, MSS Additional 36999, Royal 17 A. XVI, Egerton 1995, Harley 2332, Stowe 880, and Lansdowne 796.

[25] Davis also makes this point, "Baking for the Common Good," at 467, 492.

[26] Fennell notes that the vocabulary used and the different ways of describing bread vary in many manuscripts ("Assize," 189–190).

figure for local practices and conditions whether using the original Latin or an English translation.[27] We should not be surprised, therefore, to find some differences in vocabulary in independent translations. For example, one copy lists prices for various weights of wastel, simnel, white, wholewheat, and multigrain bread, rather than the wastel, cocket, simnel, wholewheat, treat, and multigrain types listed in the Assize.[28]

The information commons allowed not only for translating the Assize, but also for conforming it to local conditions, and this combination appears to have resulted in an entirely fictional "statute," the Statute of Winchester. The Statute of Winchester has no resemblance to the list of laws concerning local and national security that are the primary preoccupations of the actual Statute of Winchester.[29] Basically an abridgment of bread laws, the Statute of Winchester appears in several manuscripts and was printed through 1580: the laws it drew from were all part of an information commons that the initial developers mined in crafting this useful variant. In modern hacker parlance, the bread laws were common: translating them into English made them open, and they circulated freely thereafter.

The 'Statute of Winchester' runs thusly:

---

[27] Davis notes that the enforcement of the Assize was very much up to local officials and local interpretation ("Baking for the Common Good," 488, 492). Bennett's study is founded on the reality that local enforcement of the Assize of Ale was based in local practice, and states that when the Assize was kept, what was at question was broadly the national assize, and more particularly local practice (Bennett, *Ale, Beer, and Brewsters,* 99).

[28] Further, I think it likely that Additional 36999's missing header or footer originally included more text, either from the Assize or the Statute of Winchester, and that its missing header included the images of loaves so frequently accompanying the Statute of Winchester.

[29] The actual Statute of Winchester can be found on SoR, I:96. Note that the English translation is based on a mid-fifteenth-century English translation, now Kew, National Archives, MS C/49/2/10.

This is the assize of all kinds of bread. Of whatever type of grain it is it shall be weighed after the farthing wastel loaf. For the simnel loaf weighs less than the wastel loaf by two shillingweight because of its boiling, and the farthing white loaf shall weigh more than the wastel loaf by two shilling weight because of its braiding, and the halfpenny wheat loaf shall weigh the same as three farthing white loaves, and the multigrain loaf shall weigh two halfpenny white loaves. The baker shall be allowed in every quarter for use of the furnace three pence, for wood three pence, for the journeymen three pence, a halfpenny for two pages, one penny for salt, a halfpenny for yeast [or starter], a halfpenny for candles, a halfpenny for the tie-dog, and all the bran to the baker's profit. And this is the Statute of Winchester.[30]

[30] I have modernized the syntax, spelling, and punctuation:

> Thys ys the syse of al maner of brede what greyne of corne so evyr yt be yt schal be weyd aftyr the ferthyng wastel for the semnel weygeth lasse than the wastel be ii s by cause of the sethynge and the ferthyng wyght lofe schal wey more than the wastel be ii s be cause of the braydyng and the halpeny wete lofe schal wey iii ferthyng wythe loffis and the lofe of al maner corne schal wey ii [halfpenny] wyth lofys and the baker schal be alowyd in every quart for fornage iii [pennies] ffor wode iii [pennies] for the jorneymen iii [pennies]. [halfpenny] ffor ii pagys i [penny] [halfpenny] ffor salt [halfpenny] for barme [halfpenny] for candel [halfpenny] ffor the teydogge [halfpenny] an al the brenne to [his] awantage. And thys ys the statuyt of wenchester.

This is a diplomatic edition based on Douce Charters 62, with consideration of copies in Harley 2332, fol. 22r and the printed pamphlet, STC 864, fol. A2v. Abbreviations have been silently expanded and small contradictions smoothed for sense. In addition to these manuscripts and printed books, there may be at least one other copy in manuscript, though it is not included here: William Forster Lloyd printed a late fifteenth-century copy from what appears to be a legal collection in manuscript at the Bodleian Library, although he gave no shelfmark and I have not been able to identify the copy. See Wil-

The Statute of Winchester contains an expansion of the basic protections for consumer and baker allowed in the Assize and other national bread laws, and is therefore a derivative of the Assize. In stratigraphic terms, the Statute of Winchester is made of material overlaid onto the Assize of Bread, and the two layers must be read together today, as they must have been in the fifteenth century. The first section outlines relative weights and prices and follows the Assize of Bread generally, but in a more finely grained way. The Statute of Winchester links many of these types of bread and their weights to processes of baking specific types of bread. The farthing wastel loaf was boiled like a bagel, and the farthing white loaf was braided, each creating not only uniquely weighted bread, but also a specific texture and appearance. The second half of the Statute of Winchester loosely translates a chapter of the actual Assize that details allowable profit for the baker. As in the first half, this second half is more finely grained than the official Assize. The Statute of Winchester details profit to be put towards baking, wood, servants, salt, yeast (or starter, as in sourdough), candles, and the "tie-dog" presumably in charge of keeping mice and vermin out of the flour and perhaps shoplifters away from the baked goods.[31] Clearly the Statute of Winchester developed layers of accretion, as did the Assize itself. The text of the Statute of Winchester demonstrates vividly that even the statutes were situated inside the information commons.

liam Forster Lloyd, *Prices of Corn in Oxford in the Beginning of the Fourteenth Century* (Cambridge, MA: Harvard University Press, 1830), 87–88. Weights and measures are usually retained in Latin abbreviations; editorial practice here is to expand them into modern English and place them in brackets. This word supplied from STC 864 and Harley 2332; Douce Charters 62 has "ferthyng" here, apparently an eyeskip. STC 864 uses "eyst." Douce Charters 62 uses "varme" but appears to mean "barme," the skim of live culture on top of brewing beer (see Middle English Dictionary [MED], "barme"), which suggests a bread starter to me. Harley 2332 uses "barme."

[31] See MED, "tei(e", [n.1]).

Wear It Out: Forms of the Assize of Bread and the Statute of Winchester

As radical as adding specifics to laws might seem to us today, the medieval information commons extended farther yet. The text of the Assize and the Statute of Winchester could be developed into a range of forms on the page. Containing both instructions and lists of numerical ratios, these complex texts put great demands on layout, and copyists developed a variety of creative responses. In this last section of the chapter I will explore four different kinds format choices made by copyists of the bread laws that illustrate the flexibility allowed in this information commons. First, we will quickly consider copies emphasizing columns over long lines of text. Second, I will introduce laws copied on rolls rather than in books. Third, we will examine several almanacs that carried their schematic design over for use with the included bread laws. Finally, we will end with the cycle of pictures added to the Statute of Winchester, the only illustrated English law in history. Each of these transformations changes the use of a copy, and constitutes another layer of accretion on the text.

In addition to vocabulary and decoration, copyists of the statutes also had to make decisions about layout. Though often unrecognized, layout influences how a text is used, and even how functional it is. For example, the Latin copy of the Assize of Bread recorded in the modern edition of the Statutes, called the *Statutes of the Realm* and prepared by the Record Commission, is a complex text. Parts are composed of sentences in paragraph form, but much of it simply lists bread types, weights, and prices, all written out in long lines. In such a format the law is difficult to read. The Record Commission's translation in the facing column is revealing: in translating the language, they also translated the format, and in the English, the sentences are organized into paragraphs and the lists into short-line list format.[32] This practical

---

[32] This base text is London, British Library, MS Cotton Claudius D. II; see SoR, I:199–200.

approach has medieval precedent, as at least some copies of the Assize reformed those lists into two columns of short lines.[33]

Their form suggests that two such "reformist" manuscripts were designed for use as ephemera: alone among the volumes examined in this book, both show that they were initially designed as rolls, rather than as codices or "books."[34] Unlike scrolls that unspool horizontally, rolls scroll vertically. Rolls are believed to have been once far more common than their extant numbers would suggest, as they were used for their easy portability (and I think inexpensive manufacture) rather than their sturdiness.[35] While we can guess that miniature statute collections were crafted for ease of transportation, because they are (or were) rolls, we can be more sure that these two copies were working texts, designed to be used frequently.[36] It is little surprise that the Assize of Bread (and

---

[33] These are Additional 36999 and Douce Charters 62. The preparer of Additional 36999 also worked out the calculations more fully than in the copy the Record Commission printed. The text of the Assize of Bread in Additional 36999 is quite close to that found in the *Statutes of the Realm*, but follows the collated text from *Liber Horn* more closely than the Record Commission's selected base text in its names for types of bread, possibly suggesting a London provenance. Additional 36999 is incomplete at both ends, and so we cannot know how perfect the wordier parts were: the paragraphs that precede and complete the statute are missing, if they were ever there at all.

[34] Additional 36999 is a roll, and Douce Charters 62 shows stitching evidence, suggesting that it used to be part of a roll. For an image of Douce Charters 62, go to http://bodley30.bodley.ox.ac.uk:8180/luna /servlet and search "Douce Charters 62."

[35] Skemer, "Private Statute Rolls," 198. It should be noted that Skemer is referring to an Exchequer-style roll, however, and not the continuous (and larger) Chancery-style roll. Additional 36999 is in the Chancery style.

[36] Miniature and very small statute collections turn up regularly in libraries. Examples I have viewed from the time period covered by this book are: Oxford, Bodleian Library, MS Douce 16, which also happens to have an English translation of the Assize of Bread added

the Statute of Winchester) would be found in such a format: these laws formed a part of everyday medieval life.

Like rolls, almanacs were once a far more common kind of medieval ephemera than extant numbers convey. Almanacs tended to be small and portable. At least some were protected originally by small cases, like analog smartphones, to survive the rigors of being worn on the person and continually perused.[37] Some were tiny codices, but an English specialty was the folded almanac, a very large sheet of parchment folded into a tiny booklet.[38] Not unlike a smartphone their burden of keeping time came to be aggregated with a mass of other short useful materials. Religious calendars marked saints days, but also the dates of Easter and movable feast days, lunar calendars, and astrological information like the zodiac chart. Some calendars included charts or short lists of kings. Almanacs also served predictive functions, and short texts or figures predicted weather, quality of crops, and health of animals. While some almanacs could contain more specialized, medical material, many did not.[39] Schematic re-

---

to the flyleaves, and MS Douce 27; Cambridge, University Library, MS Additional 2827, MS Dd 15. 18, MS Ii 6. 10, and MS Ii 6. 25.

[37] Despite how ordinary such books must once have been, almanacs are little studied. The following introduction is based on P.R. Robinson, "'Lewdecalendars' from Lynn," in *Tributes to Kathleen L. Scott: English Medieval Manuscripts: Readers, Makers, and Illuminators,* ed. Marlene Villaloboss Hennessy (Turnhout: Harvey Miller, 2009), 221–230, and John B. Friedman, "Harry the Hayward and Talbot his Dog: An Illustrated Girdlebook from Worcestershire," in *Art into Life: Collected Papers from the Kresge Art Museum Medieval Symposia,* eds. Carol Garrett Fischer and Kathleen L. Scott (East Lansing: Michigan State University Press, 1995), 115–153. For examples of these cases, see Hilary M. Carey, "What is the Folded Almanac? The Form and Function of a Key Manuscript Source for Astro-medical Practice in Later Medieval England," *Society History of Medicine* 16 (2003): 490 [482–509].

[38] Carey argues that the folded almanacs were an English innovation ("What is the Folded Almanac?" 502).

[39] For information on medical almanacs, and the difficulty in ascertaining which count as such and which do not, see Carey, "What is

tellings of biblical texts and short prayers could appear in almanacs, as could charts of weights and measures.

Like smartphones, almanacs were densely visual texts: light on words they were heavy with numbers, charts, pictures, and icons through which users navigated to find and make use of each text. Though the iconic images might seem entirely opaque to us today, they were originally chosen for their simplicity and the ease with which they conveyed their frequently unwritten, or heavily abbreviated texts. Indeed, the Assize of Bread (and sometimes the Statute of Winchester), particularly its more abstract lists of numbers and ratios, fit into an almanac layout better than any other setting.

Reminding us of the normality of the information commons in late medieval England, a small group of almanacs remaining today are all based on the same text.[40] This alone is an extraordinary coincidence. These almanacs concentrate on astronomical science, and while miniature, nearly every page is full of carefully drawn charts and images.[41] One of the texts common to each of the almanacs in the set is the Assize of Bread. Originally the Assize in these three late fourteenth- and early fifteenth-century almanacs included no text at all, reducing the Assize of Bread to an abstract table of numbers sometimes topped by very basic depictions of loaves, and in one case, a set of scales.[42]

---

the Folded Almanac?" and Hilary M. Carey, "Astrological Medicine and the Medieval English Folded Almanac," *Social History of Medicine* 17 (2004): 345–363.

[40] Friedman claims that the other almanacs discussed here were modeled directly on Rawlinson D. 939 ("Harry the Hayward," 132).

[41] For non-legal materials in almanacs, see Friedman and Robinson generally. For images of several of the almanacs discussed here, see http://www.bl.uk/manuscripts/Default.aspx, a digitization of London, British Library, MS Harley 2332.

[42] Rawlinson D. 939, Section 4, recto; Royal 17 A XVI, fol. 23; and Harley 2332, fol. 21v. The Royal manuscript does not include images, just the chart of numbers. While two of the three almanacs are small codices, Rawlinson D. 939 is an enormous set of connected sheets that was designed to fold down to pocketsize. London, British

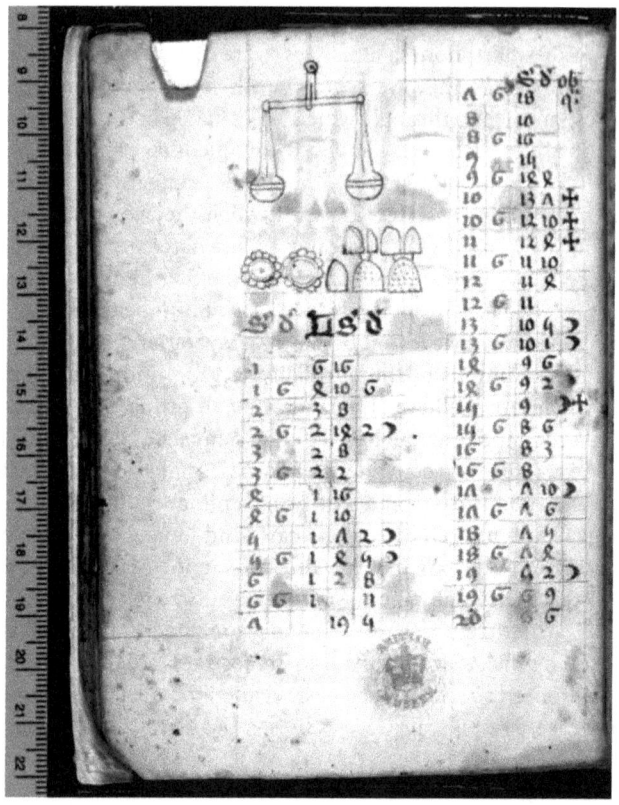

Figure 1. © De Agostini / The British Library Board London, British Library MS Harley 2332, fol. 21v. Assize of Bread Table.

The lack of text associated with the Assize of Bread in almanacs sometimes worked against it and the "worn out" statute was "renewed" with the addition of textual explanation: the Statute of Winchester. The final text originally in

Library, MS Sloane 1313 is another medical anthology that includes a single statute concerning bread, but this one is the Statute Concerning Bakers, and the entire anthology is in Latin.

one of these almanacs was the Assize of Bread, and at some point a reader determined that the Assize required updating and "made do." This page is described as a "table . . . of weights and measures": however, we can be more specific.[43] This abstract table is an almost precisely copied set of ratios drawn from the Assize of Bread, one laid out in a tabular form far more severe than either roll discussed earlier (Fig. 1). The color of the inks, style of the accompanying drawings, and ruling all suggest that this table was planned as part of this almanac, and it resembles those of the other two related almanacs.[44] However, in time this almanac's very economy of text appears to have worked against it, and the Assize table was "completed" a few decades later.

A later owner of this manuscript apparently found that the table no longer functioned well as it stood. In a hasty hand, the fifteenth-century owner added the Statute of Winchester in English on the leaf following the bread table. Clearly the volume could be seen to need text to complete the chart in order to be useful. In this instance the metaphor of geologic accretion is almost physically realized. Of interest to us is that the text selected to complete the table was this standard, but colloquial, "statute" rather than selections from the textual portions of the Assize of Bread itself. Neither text replaced the other, but both coexisted in the information commons.

The formal variety exhibited by the translations of the Assize of Bread and Statute of Winchester is wide, and indicates just how broad the information commons was. Examples of relatively light development exist, showing simple translation only. Other examples display more radical modification, including linguistic and textual transformation, and, in the almanacs in particular, significant alteration in form.

---

[43] *Catalogue of Illuminated Manuscripts,* http://collectbritain.co.uk/catalogues/illuminatedmanuscripts/record.asp?MSID=8837&ColID=8&NStart=2332 (accessed May 18, 2014).

[44] Nevertheless, Rawlinson D. 939 uses an arrangement of circles and minims as units of number rather than arabic numerals.

The developers responsible for this range of changes show no hesitation, but rather a confident creativity and exuberance in the face of textual and formal challenges. Perhaps the most striking change of all was the addition of pictures.

PICTURING THE LAW

At the same time as the Assize and the Statute of Winchester appear in almanacs, the bread laws demonstrate another formal experiment: illustrations. European law was thoroughly illustrated, and standard visual programs had developed long before the fifteenth century.[45] In contrast, law in England was stultifyingly plain. Though some legal manuscripts showed beautifully illuminated borders and initials, the only "pictures" they included were invariably kings seated in judgment. Therefore, the illustrations added to the Assize of Bread and the Statute of Winchester were entirely unique.

Unlike any other English law, in translation the Assize of Bread and its customary variant the Statute of Winchester appear to have come to carry a simple visual program that appears in multiple manuscripts, and successfully moved into print. One of the roll copies of the Statute of Winchester illustrates traditional iconography for this "Statute": depictions of a sack of grain and various loaves of bread (Fig. 2). Similar, though far simpler loaves are depicted in the almanacs that we discussed above.[46] Beginning with a pamphlet printed in the late 1520s, these complex loaves continue to be associated with the Assize of Bread and the Statute of Win-

---

[45] For recent discussion of Continental and canon law illustration, see Susan L'Engle and Robert Gibbs, *Illuminating the Law: Legal Manuscripts in Cambridge Collections* (Turnhout: Harvey Miller, 2001) and accompanying website: http://www.fitzmuseum.cam.ac.uk/gallery/law/. And for a probing exploration into the relationship between Continental law and images, see Marta Madero, *Tabula Picta: Painting and Writing in Medieval Law*, trans. Monique Dascha Inciarte and Roland David Valayre (Philadelphia: University of Pennsylvania Press, 2009).

[46] Harley 2332; Royal 17. A. XVI; Rawlinson D. 939.

chester until the 1580s. Of note is the standardization of the iconography. In all of the manuscripts and the printed pamphlet, at least one of the smaller loaves is always circular and ringed about with semi-circles or dots, and this pattern seems to relate to the traditional design of this type of bread. In one of the almanacs, catalogers have identified these shapes as weights. If that is true for the abstract almanac images, then the shapes of the weights used to assay the bread were based on the shapes of the types of bread. The roll's images and the printed pamphlet are detailed enough to be clear that each depicts the loaves themselves, and not simply the weights used for weighing bread. Whether adding functionality for the less literate or simply adding decoration to an otherwise stark legal text, these pictures add to the ways in which these statutes were reformatted when they were translated. In recycling the Statute of Winchester the hackers also renewed it.

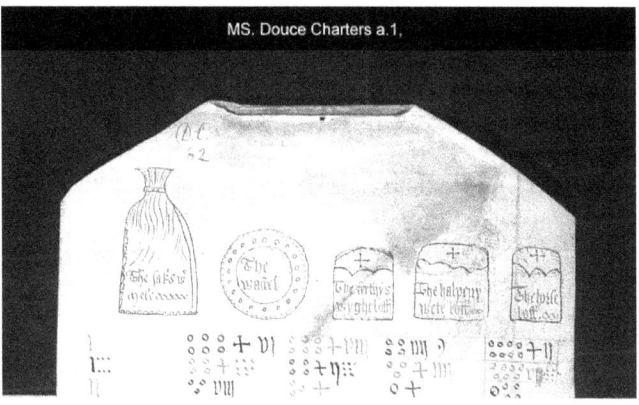

Figure 2. The Bodleian Libraries, The University of Oxford, Douce Charters a. 1. no. 62, Bread loaves

If illustrations might be seen to "open" a text to a wider readership, one final kind of illustration opened the volume in a physical way. Beginning with a pamphlet printed in the 1520s, for most of the sixteenth century the Assize of Bread and the Statute of Winchester bore an illustrated title page, a "cover," if you will.[47] This title page shows a series of four woodcuts depicting baking and assaying bread (and the dog), and these continued to be used in subsequent editions (Fig. 3). Together with the cover images, the illustrations of the loaves in this pamphlet are unheard of in a printed English law book. The illustrations, coupled with the accessible translations appear to have been a successful marketing strategy and this remarkable pamphlet remained in print until 1580.[48] Through most of the sixteenth century, this pamphlet of bread laws would have been very common indeed.

Each of these derivatives demonstrates the medieval information commons in action in several respects. Both official and hacked traditional texts circulated and were copied freely, and they were modified to update them or to fit them to local needs. Texts could be added to or subtracted from almanacs, depending on an individual user's needs and interests. Over time, the highly abstract form of the Assize of Bread used in almanacs appears to have become confusing, perhaps as the popularity of the Statute of Winchester grew. In short, the Assize of Bread and the Statute of Winchester both manifest the information commons characteristic of manuscript culture.

If the statute law was more controlled than any other kind of text, then the variety of modifications made to it prove that the information commons was simply the status quo for

[47] My policy below will be to give complete citations for texts I discuss in the chapter, and STC numbers alone for simple references. STC 864: "Here begynnethe the boke named the assyse of bread what it ought to waye after the pryce of a quarter of wheete," Richard Bankes [London, not after 1532]. For more discussion of this pamphlet, see Kathleen E. Kennedy, "A London Legal Miscellany, Popular Law, and Medieval Print Culture," in *Truth and Tales: Cultural Mobility and Medieval Media*, eds. Nicholas Watson and Fiona Somerset (Columbus: Ohio State University Press, 2015).

[48] STC 866 (Robert Wyer, 1544?), STC 867 (Wyer, 1546?), STC 868.2 (Wyer, 1553?), STC 868.4 (Wyer, 1555?), STC 868.6 (Colwell/Wyer, ca.1560), STC 868.8 (Colwell, 1570), STC 869.5 (Jackson, 1580), and STC 869 (Jackson, 1580).

medieval England. This commons forms a bedrock layer beneath textual cultures built on that of medieval England, including our own. Clearly the modern topography of broadly construed copyright and shrinking fair use in no way resembles its deepest substratum. Yet the information commons persists here and there, as we saw in Chapter 1, and we can see these instance as this medieval bedrock emerging into the modern textual landscape. Not identical to medieval information commons, time and exposure have changed this stratum when we see it today, as with any exposed artifact. Project Gutenberg and Wikipedia are notably different than medieval statute manuscripts, and smartphones are not medieval almanacs.

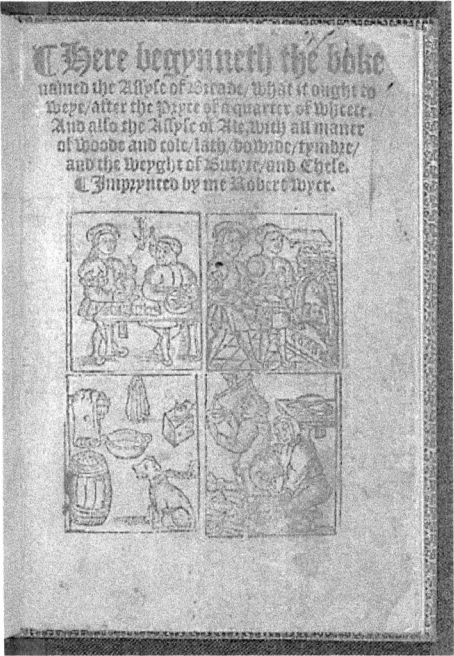

Figure 3. © De Agostini / The British Library Board, London, British Library, C.28.d.3, fol. A1r. Illustrations accompanying the so-called Statute of Winchester.

There were no institutional attempts to control this medieval practice of translating and reforming statutes, just as there were no attempts to control the copying and transforming of literary texts. However, the medieval information commons was not to last. Later, in Chapter 5, we will see the law printers themselves endeavor to control who could translate and print statutes, and they ask for and receive royal assistance in so doing. In Chapter 3, we will consider a failed attempt at such institutional control over the information commons, as the Wycliffite Bible came to be both illegal and a bestseller. It appears that hackers develop an identity and express their common values at such moments of institutional coercion.

CHAPTER 3: THE FIRST HACKER BIBLE

Like literature and law, the Bible was part of the medieval information commons, and therefore part of the bedrock of our current media culture. As did so many Europeans, the medieval English enjoyed a long tradition of bible translation. In medieval England, the Bible's text functioned as an information commons and anyone could borrow from it. Yet, it was bible translation that proved to be the firing point for the beginnings of a proprietary information culture. Archbishop Thomas Arundel attempted to outlaw bible translation in England in 1409. Named for John Wyclif, an Oxford theologian and posthumously declared heretic, the collaborative bible translation known as the Wycliffite Bible was the first complete Bible in English and drew the balance of Arundel's ire. At least one of the translators and editors who worked on the Wycliffite Bible was concerned enough about the larger implications of Arundel's rights grab that he penned a work that today stands as the first statement of hacker values. This author argued for the commonness, openness, and freedom of biblical text in the face of Arundel's attempt to render it proprietary. Nevertheless, the threat against this portion of the information commons was not realized effectively in the fifteenth century and instead the Wycliffite Bible "went viral," laying down a thick layer of media sediment and stifling all previous translations. Today the Wycliffite Bible remains by far the most plentiful Middle English text.[1] The Wycliffite Bible may have been an open source project that elicited the first expression of hacker ideals but the translation turned out to be so popular that this defensive posture was unnecessary.

The layers of this chapter will progress from oldest and lowest to higher and newer. First, I will make a case for bible translation as evidence for an information commons in medieval England, as I did in Chapter 2 with statute law. Attempts at effacing this stratum were made by Arundel and others, however, and the middle portion of the chapter will explore evidence of this attempt at cultural change. Although Arundel's efforts proved to be ineffective, they were noticed by at least some translators and editors. One self-conscious response to Arundel's agenda forms the final section of this chapter.

---

[1] About 265 whole or partial copies remain, nearly double that of any other text in Middle English. See Mary Dove, *The First English Bible: Text and Context of the Wycliffite Versions* (Cambridge, UK: Cambridge University Press, 2007), for the most recent, most complete listing of Wycliffite Bible manuscripts. The *Brut* is the second-most plentiful remaining book, with 180 copies: see Lister Matheson, *The Prose Brut: the Development of a Middle English Chronicle* (Tempe, AZ: Medieval and Renaissance Texts and Studies, 1998), 6. More nearly comparable to the Wycliffite Bible is *Prick of Conscience,* of which 155 manuscripts remain: see Robert E. Lewis and Angus McIntosh, *A Descriptive Guide to the Manuscripts of the Prick of Conscience* (Oxford: Society for the Study of Mediaeval Languages and Literature, 1982), 1. I count the English Books of Hours in this number: Kathleen E. Kennedy, "Reintroducing the English Books of Hours, or 'English Primers'," *Speculum* 89 (2014): 693–723.

THE BIBLE AS A TRADITIONAL INFORMATION COMMONS

As a derivative, a translation, the Wycliffite Bible was hugely popular and its spread was so wide that it effectively overlaid all previous bible translations, creating a durable new cultural stratum. In software we speak of a "category killer," a product so excellent that nothing can surpass it until conditions change, and the Wycliffite Bible was such a product. The Wycliffite Bible saturated the market for bible translation. The verb "saturated" suggests water, and we should think of the sediment that travels in moving water and that settles eventually to create new layers of earth. Like sediment, the Wycliffite Bible covered what came before thoroughly and imposed a unity where there had been diversity. Yet it did this, apparently, by beating the competition in the marketplace, not because it was supported by an institution.

As Ralph Hanna has amply demonstrated, hacking biblical texts was a passion of the later medieval English; it was a tradition.[2] Hanna explores the tradition of bible translation in later medieval England at length, and in the end determines that the Wycliffite Bible "became a full substitute and drove out . . . competing biblical versions."[3] By expanding "bible translation" to its widest limits, including paraphrase, versification, commentary, apocrypha, and even considering literature with a heavy scriptural background, Hanna demonstrates that from the beginning of the fourteenth century translated scripture was at the heart of English literary culture. Among the earliest examples of London Middle English are manuscripts that provide "reasonably direct access to biblical texts," and Hanna goes so far as to consider prose bible translation as "one centre of the early London booktrade."[4] Hanna rests his conviction concerning changes in

---

[2] Ralph Hanna, *London Literature, 1300-1380* (Cambridge, UK: Cambridge University Press, 2005), throughout, but especially Chapter 4.
[3] Hanna, *London Literature,* 310.
[4] Hanna, *London Literature,* 7, 9.

English literary culture in the late fourteenth century on the Wycliffite Bible: "the very fidelity to the Latin text and the absence of sectarian additions . . . made the book useful to a general interested audience" and he argues that in the fifteenth century the Wycliffite Bible largely supplanted the richly diverse biblical texts that preceded it.[5]

METAMORPHIC SCRIPTURE

In geologic metamorphosis, rock undergoes physical change, sometimes at a chemical level, due to pressure and temperature changes. We might think of texts in the information commons as liable to undergoing such physical alteration, and scripture translation offers a range of examples of this metamorphosis. The shift from a plethora of scriptural translations to a narrowed selection that Hanna uncovers can be illustrated using the psalms. Four different English translations of some or all of the psalms circulated in fifteenth-century England, together with an English translation of the psalms in the Book of Hours based on the Wycliffite Bible, and of course the Wycliffite Bible itself. All treated the text of the Bible as common, open, and free. All of these versions of the psalms are hacked, much like the statutes we studied in the previous chapter. The variation in the four translations is broad, suggesting that there were few limits on this information commons. Nevertheless, the overwhelmingly popular translation was the Wycliffite translation: it was idiomatic, and unlike the rest, capable of being read on its own, without commentary.

Three of the translations represent varying levels of paraphrase and produce metamorphic derivatives of the psalms, that is, psalms mixed with other material and formed anew under pressure. Richard Maidstone, Thomas Brampton, and John Lydgate all wrote versions of psalms that date to the very late fourteenth or early fifteenth centuries. All three were likely clergy. Lydgate's psalm translations show the wid-

---

[5] Hanna, *London Literature,* 310.

est range and run the gamut from pure allusion to close literal translation.⁶ Maidstone's editor, Valerie Edden suggests that subsequent copyists felt free to revise his psalms to fit their own purposes, and I would add that this is consonant with treating the Bible as an information commons.⁷ Ultimately, the freedom to produce and to copy these translations into the Tudor period argues that the Bible was a traditional information commons for the medieval English.

The manuscript tradition of these paraphrases show widely varying treatment: few copies are complete, and many include only one or a few psalms⁸ Control of even the form of the text was impossible: in Brampton's poem, the presence of the Latin text of the psalms appears to be optional: some manuscripts include the Latin verses together with the English paraphrase and some do not.⁹ Most of these psalm trans-

---

⁶ For the text of them, see Henry Macracken, *The Minor Poems of John Lydgate*, Vol. 1 (Oxford: Oxford University Press, 1911).

⁷ For bibliography on Maidstone's psalms, see Lynn Staley, "The Penitential Psalms: Conversion and the Limits of Lordship," *Journal of Medieval and Early Modern Studies* 37 (2007): 261n7 [221–269], and Valerie Edden, *Richard Maidstone's Pentitential Psalms edited from Oxford, Bodleian Library, MS Rawlinson A 389* (Heidelburg: Carl Winter, 1990), 21.

⁸ Of the twenty-seven manuscripts containing Maidstone's paraphrase, only six contain the entire thing, and together the manuscripts illustrate three significantly different versions of the poem (Edden, *Penitential Psalms*, 20–21). Brampton's paraphrase is known through only seven copies. For bibliography on Brampton's psalms, see Staley, "Penitential Psalms," 265n49, 265n58, and Michael Kuczynski, *Prophetic Song: The Psalms as Moral Discourse in Late Medieval England* (Philadelphia: University of Pennsylvania Press, 1995), 125–135. Lydgate's psalms are known in only three or four copies each: see Macracken, *Minor Poems*, 1, and Margaret Connolly, *John Shirley: Book Production and the Noble Household in Fifteenth-Century England* (Aldershot, UK: Ashgate, 1998), 178–179.

⁹ London, British Library, MS Sloane 1853 includes them. MS Sloane 1853 can be found at: http://collectbritain.co.uk/catalogues/ illuminatedmanuscripts/searchMSNo.asp, by searching for "Sloane

lations were copied into religious and devotional anthologies. In one manuscript not far from his copy of Lydgate's Psalm 102, John Shirley copied Brampton's Penitential Psalms.[10] Maidstone's poem often turns up next to works by, or attributed to, Richard Rolle, an earlier scripture translator. Both Brampton and Maidstone occur alone in pamphlet form only occasionally.[11] The decoration of these anthologies ranges from luxuriously illuminated, to finely flourished, plainer copies, to un-illuminated, un-flourished copies.[12]

A group of Books of Hours illustrates another way in which biblical text might be metamorphosed, in this case translating a popular prayer-book and inserting text derived from the Wycliffite Bible itself. The fourteenth century saw the development of the Book of Hours, an outgrowth of the psalter that became the most popular book of the late Middle Ages in England as on the Continent.[13] The core devotion of

---

1853." Cambridge, Cambridge University Library, MS Ff. 2. 38 does not include them.

[10] Cambridge, Trinity College, MS R. 3. 20. See Connolly, *John Shirley,* Table 2, 73.

[11] Sloane 1853 (a finely flourished copy of Brampton) and Oxford, Bodleian Library, Douce MS 232 (Maidstone). For images of Douce 232, go to http://bodley30.bodley.ox.ac.uk:8180/luna/servlet and search "Douce 232."

[12] See, for example, San Marino, Huntington Library, MS HM 142, which includes Maidstone's paraphrase. See images via the catalog entry here: http://sunsite.berkeley.edu/hehweb/HM142.html. For a plain example, see Douce 232, a pamphlet containing Maidstone's poem. For a sample image, see note 11 above.

[13] For accessible introductions, see Roger S. Wieck, "The Book of Hours," in *The Liturgy of the Medieval Church,* eds. Thomas J. Heffernan and E. Ann Matter (Kalamazoo, MI: Medieval Institute Publications, 2001), 473–513, and Mary C. Erler, "Devotional Literature," in *The Cambridge History of the Book in Britain, Vol. 3: 1400-1557,* eds. Lotte Hellinga and J.B. Trapp (Cambridge, UK: Cambridge University Press, 1999), 495–525. For the foundational treatment, see Victor Leroquais, *Les livres d'heures manuscrits de la Bibliothèque Nationale de Paris* (Paris: Protat, 1927). For the development of Books of Hours, see Bella Millett, "Ancrene Wisse and

the Book of Hours was the Hours of the Virgin and this consisted mostly of psalms. I have argued elsewhere that sixteen copies of the Book of Hours translated into English make use of versions of the Wycliffite Bible for their psalms.[14] Psalms make up approximately 77% of the text of the Book of Hours, and so all of these volumes are made up mostly of the Wycliffite Bible.[15] In Books of Hours we see the Wycliffite Bible treated as common and used freely thanks to the translators who had opened the Latin text into English. Whatever their religious beliefs, the developers of the English Hours made use of a popular scripture translation to speed their development of a derivative of a different popular text, the Book of Hours.

Manuscript evidence argues for the Bible continuing to be an information commons throughout the fifteenth century in the face of attempts at institutional control.[16] In the end, we can turn to a Latin Book of Hours containing Maidstone's paraphrase of the Penitential Psalms to argue for the commonness of, even appreciation for, such metamorphic scriptural texts.[17] This volume features fine illuminated borders

---

the Book of Hours," in *Writing Religious Women: Female Spirituality and Textual Practices in Late Medieval England,* eds. Denis Renevey and Christiana Whitehead (Toronto: University of Toronto Press, 2000), 21–40. See Wieck's and Erler's references for a more detailed bibliography on the topic.

[14] This section of the chapter is based on these publications: Kathleen E. Kennedy, *Courtly and Commercial Art of the Wycliffite Bible* (Turnhout: Brepols, 2014) and Kennedy, "Reintroducing the English Books of Hours."

[15] Christopher de Hamel, "Books of Hours 'Imaging' the Word," in *The Bible as Book: The Manuscript Tradition,* eds. John Sharpe III and Kimberly van Kampen (London: British Library, 1998), 138 [137–143].

[16] Henry Ansgar Kelly argues for the relative mildness of the Constitutions, but also notes that local bishops sometimes interpreted it in stringent ways the original wording does not support, see Henry Ansgar Kelly, *Inquisitions and Other Trial Procedures in the Medieval West* (Aldershot, UK: Ashgate, 2001), Sec. VI , 279–303.

[17] New York, Morgan Library, MS M. 99.

and an occasional historiated initial all executed by artists in Gloucester, likely at the Abbey of St. Peter.[18] Important for this chapter is the replacement of the usual Latin Penitential Psalms with Maidstone's English paraphrase. This English replacement text is highlighted by a sumptuous, nearly half-page historiated initial by the Oriel Master.[19] There is no shyness or hesitancy about swapping English paraphrase for the Latin text here: the information commons is visible in this Book of Hours, and attention is called to it with an arresting miniature. Clearly the scriptural information commons was healthy in the fifteenth century, but changes were also in the air.

Defending Richard Rolle's Intellectual Property

The fourth version of the psalms—and the most popular before the Wycliffite Bible—was rendered by the fourteenth-century hermit Richard Rolle.[20] Rolle's translation of the psalms predated Wyclif and so according to the Constitutions of Arundel (1407-1409) that outlawed the Wycliffite Bible, Rolle's translations were technically legal throughout

---

[18] See the box notes to the volume, available online: http://corsair.morganlibrary.org/msdescr/BBM0099.htm. See also Scott's notes to the related volume Oxford, Bodleian Library, MS Digby 233 and others decorated by these artists: *Later Gothic Manuscripts, 1390-1490*, 2 vols. (New York: Harvey Miller, 1996), II:124, 126.

[19] Morgan M. 99, fol. 92r. Scott, *Later Gothic*, II:126–127, identifies this artist as the Oriel Master.

[20] More than thirty copies remain today. See Dorothy Everett, "The Middle English Prose Psalter of Richard Rolle of Hampole," *Modern Language Review* 17 (1922): 217 [217–227]. Nicholas Watson says "nearly forty manuscripts" of the *English Psalter* exist: *Richard Rolle and The Invention of Authority* (Cambridge, UK: Cambridge University Press, 1991), 242. The *English Psalter* is beginning to be published in a modern edition by Anne Hudson, and the first volume is now available as *Two Revisions of Richard Rolle's English Psalter Commentary and Related Canticles* (Oxford: Oxford University Press, 2013).

the fifteenth century. The *English Psalter* is itself a text illustrating stratification, as it includes each psalm line in Latin, followed by Rolle's strictly literal English translation (Nicholas Watson calls the translation "manifestly not self-sufficient"), followed by Rolle's commentary explicating each verse.[21]

As we might expect, Rolle's *English Psalter* was itself treated as part of an information commons, and about half of the manuscripts we have today include interpolations, or additions by subsequent readers.[22] Michael Kuczynski and Kevin Gustafson find it entirely likely that some of the interpolators saw their revisions as of a piece with Rolle's own work.[23] Some interpolations encourage the believer through a time of persecution. Kucyznski connects this type of psalm hacking with identification with the psalmist himself in his own persecution.[24] Gustafson sees oversight as the crucial impossibility, as "any such text could become a vehicle for heterodoxy," and "readers . . . [were] making the text so dangerously unstable."[25] The multiplicity of potential readings shows how the biblical text functions like a spiritual tool, as in most instances the audience determined the relative orthodoxy of the reading. As with open source code today, once

---

[21] Watson, *Richard Rolle*, 246.
[22] Everett, "Middle English Prose Psalter," 218, and Michael Kuczynski, "Rolle Among the Reformers: Orthodoxy and Heterodoxy in Wycliffite Copies of Richard Rolle's *English Psalter*," in *Mysticism and Spirituality in Medieval England,* eds. William Pollard and Robert Boenig (Cambridge, UK: Boydell & Brewer, 1997), 177n3 [177–202].
[23] Kuczynski questions Everett's identification of many "Wycliffite" interpolated passages, saying that in the context of Augustinian psalm commentary on one hand, and Wycliffite psalm glosses on the other, many additions to the *English Psalter* previously identified as Lollard appear to be orthodox (Kuczynski, "Rolle Among the Reformers," 195).
[24] Kuczynski, "Rolle Among the Reformers," 199.
[25] Kevin Gustafson, "Richard Rolle's English Psalter and the Making of a Lollard Text," *Viator* 33 (2002): 296–297, 299 [294–309].

a text was released, it could be variously developed, and a text left as open as Rolle's "tantalizingly ambiguous" *English Psalter* could be developed in many different directions that could then be interpreted in many different ways.[26] In other words, editors simply took a useful common text and further developed it. Furthermore, these editors followed what would be considered good hacker etiquette today and attributed the original to Rolle.[27]

At the same time as copyists felt comfortable developing Rolle's text, a new sense of a fixed, proprietary text was also beginning to manifest. Surely this is related to the developing notion of what it means to be an author, of intellectual property as we know it, and to burgeoning humanism, spreading from Italy through France and reaching into England in Wyclif's lifetime. Wyclif and his followers tangled desperately with theologian Jean Gerson, who may well have developed the notion of a "public intellectual" and who exercised an unusual control over the dissemination of his own works.[28] I do not mean to suggest here that Gerson's ideas drove the attempt to control texts directly, but both directly through activity on pan-European Church councils and indirectly through his writing, Gerson and other scholars were developing and spreading new ideas about the importance of fixed, inalterable texts.

In evidence that such ideas were filtering into England in this period, a preface added to one copy of Rolle's *English Psalter* asserts that Rolle's translation is not common but proprietary. This preface emphasizes the care that Rolle took with his translation, links Rolle's writing with his miracles,

---

[26] Gustafson, "English Psalter," 302.

[27] Kuczynski, *Prophetic Song*, 166, 170–171. Eric S. Raymond notes this ascription as part of the hacker ethos: *The Cathedral and the Bazaar: Musings on Linux and Open Source by an Accidental Revolutionary* (New York: O'Reilly, 1999), 88–89.

[28] For the recent, magisterial consideration of Gerson's career, see Daniel Hobbins, *Authorship and Publicity Before Print: Jean Gerson and Transformation of Late Medieval Learning* (Philadelphia: University of Pennsylvania Press, 2009).

and emphasizes that anyone altering Rolle's text was acting like a heretic, like a Lollard, or follower of Wyclif.[29] The author of the preface argues that to revise the *English Psalter* is not illegal, but impious. While Rolle himself seems to have been sanguine about the openness of manuscript tradition, this prefacer attempts to claim the *Psalter* as Rolle's intellectual property, and therefore cuts against the grain of tradition.

In the preface, Rolle's position as a Jerome-like holy, learned translator is emphasized in a characterization that Kuczynski calls God's "scribe-prophet."[30] Rolle "glossed the psalter that follows in English expertly."[31] Included in a list of Rolle's miraculous accomplishments is making "many a holy book."[32] The prefacer describes Rolle again as a sort of Jerome when he says "this holy man expounds: he follows the holy doctors of the Church;/ And in all his Englishing; he follows the Latin text./ And makes his translation complete: short, good, and profitable/ for men's souls."[33] Rolle is not creating anything new here, the prefacer claims, but closely follows standard commentaries ("holy doctors of the

---

[29] Oxford, Bodleian Library, MS Laud Misc. 286. See Gustafson, "English Psalter," 295. For a digitized image of fol. 1r discussed below, go to http://bodley30.bodley.ox.ac.uk:8180/luna/servlet and search for "Laud Misc. 286." Nevertheless, even Gustafson recommends caution: lacking complete modern editions of either the *English Psalter* or Rolle's earlier *Latin Psalter,* and given the range of "Lollard" beliefs, identifying "Lollard" interpolations with any accuracy is a risky project indeed ("English Psalter," 297).

[30] Kuczynski, "Rolle Among the Reformers," 179.

[31] "Glosed the sauter that sues here in englysch tongue sykerly," line 23. I quote from Bramley's edition of the metrical preface, checked against the digital image of lines 1–44 of the preface on the Bodleian's website. See Henry Bramley, *The Psalter: Or Psalms of David and Certain Canticles* (Oxford: Clarendon, 1884).

[32] "Many a holy boke," line 37.

[33] "This holy man in expownyng: he fologth holy doctours;/ And in all hys englysching: ry3t aftur the latyn taketh cours./ And makes it compendyous: short gode and profetabul/ To mannys soule," lines 41–44.

Church") in his exegesis and the Latin in his biblical translation. The result is "complete," or all a pious reader could need: short, good, and profitable.

For the prefacer, Rolle's learning and holiness prevented the hermit from doing harm to Jerome's text just as medieval tradition had it that Jerome's learning and holiness prevented him from doing harm to biblical text. Therefore the prefacer cautions that anyone else amending Rolle's work was doing wrong: "there is no error in it: nor any deceit or heresy,/ But every word is solid as stone: and is absolute truth/ Whoever will copy this I advise him: copy carefully line by line,/ And write no more than is here written: or else I tell him, not you it will not be right."[34] The holy text, expounded by a holy man is compendious and perfect, fixed like a stone: a secure, true textual act. Copying such a text ought not be undertaken lightly, but be done carefully. No mention is made of abbreviation. The prefacer is apparently afraid only of expansion.

Note here how even this restriction of the commons fails to reach the level of control characteristic of modern intellectual property. The prefacer allows, even encourages copying, in a way foreign to current law. However, as today, no derivation is to be made: copyists must acknowledge Rolle's masterful work, and replicate it perfectly without adding anything. In fact, the prefacer describes a situation not unlike the rights and limitations contained in the license on this present book, a Creative Commons Attribution-NonCommerical-No-Derivs 3.0 Unported License. Today that license is considered progressive and advocates a publishing process more open than normal. When the prefacer wrote, his stance was progressive and advocated a dissemination process more proprietary than normal.

The "error," "deceit," and "heresy" the prefacer references are directly linked with textual expansion associated with an

---

[34] "Errour in hit is ther non: ne deseyt ne heresy,/ Bot euery word is sad as stone: and sothly sayd, ful sykerly/ Whos wol it write I rede hym rygth: wryte on warly lyne be lyne,/ And make no more then here is dygth: or ellys I rede hym hit ne ryne," lines 45–48.

evangelical lollardy making free use of common texts:

> This Psalter has been copied by evil men of lollardy:/ And afterward it has been seen to be engrafted with heresy./ They said then to uneducated fools that this Psalter is in its entirety/ A blessed book of their schools: Richard of Hampole's Psalter!/ This they claim craftily to make people believe their teachings/ To reel them in, and in so doing destroy them, against the faith, a great foolishness/ And slander this holy man foully with their crafty, wicked wiles.[35]

As Kuczynski notes, "to be grafted into" connotes a slicing of heresy into the holy man's text.[36] Adding insult to injury, the prefacer blames the Lollards for claiming Rolle's book as one of their own, using the holy man's book and his brand, his name, to lure in the unsuspecting to heretical conversion. Here we have intellectual property anxiety clearly expressed. For the prefacer, anyone making changes to Rolle's text, any hackers, are pirates, Lollards, and heretics. Ironically, the text of this copy of the *English Psalter* is itself an interpolated text (though not clearly a heretical one).[37] Despite his desire to do so, the prefacer could not fence the psalms: they were an information commons and audiences ensured that they circulated freely.

THE VIRAL WYCLIFFITE BIBLE

The tradition of the Bible as an information commons re-

---

[35] "Copyed has this Sauter ben: of yuel men of lollardry:/ And afturward hit has bene sene: ympyd in with eresy./ They seyden then to leude foles: that it shuld be all enter,/ A blessyd boke of hur scoles: of Rychard Hampole the Sauter./ Thus thei seyde to make theim leue: on her scole thoro sotelte:/ To bryng hem in, so hem to greue: ageyn the feyth in grete fole:/ And slaundird foule this holy man: with her wykkyd waryed wyles," lines 51–55.
[36] Kucyznski, "Rolle Among the Reformers," 179–180.
[37] Kuczynski, "Rolle Among the Reformers," 180, notes this irony.

ceived a direct challenge early in the fifteenth century and the prefacer of Rolle's *English Psalter* offers evidence that this challenge met with some support. In Archbishop Thomas Arundel's infamous Constitutions of 1407-1409, translating the Bible or reading such a translation could lead to one being suspected of heresy.[38] Contemporary events led to the moment in Article 7 of the Constitutions when Arundel claimed the English Church's property rights over the text of the Bible, and denied anyone the right "by his owne authoritie, [to] translate any text of the Scripture into English" and demanded "that no man read any such boke."[39] No mere flash in the pan would have goaded Arundel into such a statement, but only a translation that was open and already circulating freely.

That Arundel could have attempted to enforce Church control over scripture is itself interesting. The Church had traditionally exercised control over the *interpretation* of scripture, but to extend interpretation to include *translation,* or derivative works, had not been attempted since Jerome. As we have seen, the Bible was part of the information commons, and had been translated and developed as long as there had been an English language. Yet whether he wrote before or after Arundel's pronouncement, the Rolle prefacer reminds us that the information commons was being reassessed more broadly in this period. Arundel put institutional

---

[38] Henry Kelly explicates these passages in the Constitutions carefully and cautions that technically the penalty was a formal suspicion of heresy, not heresy itself. See Kelly, *Inquisitions*, Sec. VI, 279–303.

[39] John Foxe, *Acts and Monuments* (London: John Day, 1570), 672. For a scholarly edition, see *Foxe's Book of Martyrs Variorum Edition Online*: http://www.johnfoxe.org (accessed May 18, 2014). The original text can be found in *Concilia Magnae Britainniae et Hiberniae*, ed. David Wilkins, 4 vols. (London, 1737), 3:317, where it reads: "statuimus igitur et ordinamus, ut nemo deinceps aliquem textum sacrae scripturae auctoritate sua in linguam Anglicanam, vel aliam transferat, per viam libri, libelli, aut tractatus nec legatur aliquis hujusmodi liber, libellus, aut tractatus jam noviter tempore dicti Johannis Wycliff."

heft behind such aspirations of control.

Unusually collaborative for its time, the Wycliffite Bible project looks to us today remarkably like an open source project. Currently there is general acceptance that, while Wyclif himself argued for the importance of bible study and that the Bible should be available in English for both clergy and laypeople, it was a group of his followers rather than himself who labored at translating the Bible into English.[40] Eric Raymond notes that modern open source projects follow a unique release pattern: they stay in beta for a long time while users and developers work together to identify and fix bugs, but when a full, official release is made, it is a solid, workable product.[41] The Wycliffite Bible follows this open source pattern, having a beta version, the Earlier Version (EV), which was "absolutely and sometimes incomprehensibly faithful to the literal sense and word-order of the Latin."[42] Scholars believe the EV to have been begun in the mid-1370s.[43] Raymond cautions that "beta software is notoriously buggy."[44] The EV was certainly "buggy," but improvements began to be made swiftly and accretively, and the more readable, more colloquial Later Version (LV) came to be the standard release. It was the LV, completed by 1400, which became the bestseller described by Hanna, and EV's copying ceased rapidly around 1400.[45] Christina von Nolcken estimates that 85

---

[40] Dove explores Wyclif's references to bible translation in detail and points out that they begin only in 1382 (*First English Bible,* 69–70).

[41] Raymond, *The Cathedral and the Bazaar,* 38–44.

[42] David Lawton, "Englishing the Bible, 1066-1549," in *The Cambridge History of Medieval English Literature,* ed. David Wallace (Cambridge, UK: Cambridge University Press, 1999), 470 [454–482].

[43] Dove, *First English Bible,* 81, and Christopher de Hamel, *The Book: A History of the Bible* (London: Phaidon Press, 2001), 173.

[44] Eric S. Raymond, *The New Hacker's Dictionary,* 3rd edn. (Cambridge, MA: M.I.T. Press, 1996), 63.

[45] Matti Peikola, "'First is writen a clause of the bigynnynge therof': The Table of Lections in the Manuscripts of the Wycliffite Bible," *Boletin Millares Carlo* 24-25 (2005-2006): 349 [343–378]; Hanna,

percent of the roughly 250 extant manuscripts contain text in LV.[46] In computer hackers' terms, the LV was the stable release, designed to "go viral."

Given the information commons out of which the Wycliffite Bible came, it may not be surprising that the LV was designed to be a broadly useful text, with an easily replicable structure. Moreover it was as ecumenical a text as could be: no one in the Middle Ages and no one today has found any heretical material in the text of the translation itself. It would appear that the diverse group of developers who gathered to accomplish this enormous task achieved a text anyone could use, regardless of religious affiliation. The LV was not copied to be hidden under a bushel.

The many extant copies prove that the Wycliffite Bible spread widely as it was copied from the late fourteenth into the early sixteenth century, and individual copies can be associated with a range of pre-Reformation owners.[47] At least eleven copies were owned by religious: monks, nuns, and priests.[48] Five copies were owned by members of the royal

---

London Literature, 310.

[46] Christina von Nolcken, "Lay Literacy, the Democratization of God's Law and the Lollards," in *The Bible as Book: The Manuscript Tradition,* eds. John Sharpe and Kimberly van Kampen (London: British Library, 1998), 180 [177–195].

[47] Most of the lists in this paragraph are drawn from Peikola, with additions of my own: see Matti Peikola, "Aspects of *Mise-en-page* in Manuscripts of The Wycliffite Bible," in *Medieval Texts in Context,* eds. Graham Cane and Denise Renevy (New York: Routledge, 2008), 60–61n19. For a recent discussion of ownership, more specifically, see Elizabeth Solopova, "Manuscript Evidence for the Patronage, Ownership and Use of the Wycliffite Bible," in *Form and Function in the Late Medieval Bible,* eds. Eyal Poleg and Laura Light (Leiden: Brill, 2013), 333–349.

[48] Alnwick Castle, MS 449 (Thetford Priory of St. George); Bel Air, CA, Dr. Steve Somer (St. Margaret's, Bridge Street, London, Thomas Downe, clerk; see Dove, *First English Bible,* 281); Cambridge, Magdalene College, MS Pepys 2073 (Prior of St. John's of Jerusalem); St. John's College, MS E. 14 (London priest); London, British Library, MSS Additional 10596 (Barking Abbey), Additional 41175

family.⁴⁹ A further four copies were owned by lesser nobility such as the gentry, or members of the wealthy urban mercantile classes.⁵⁰ This by no means exhausts the list of known owners. In addition, copies that no longer exist are recorded in wills, inventories, and library lists.⁵¹ The extant, signed copies show a geographical spread from Newcastle in the north, Norwich in the east, Shrewsbury in the west, and the Isle of Wight in the south. By the early sixteenth century a copy of the Wycliffite Bible had been translated into Scots.⁵² There is nowhere the Wycliffite Bible did not go, and like a layer of sediment spread by a relentless flood it reached across the length and breadth of the island's media culture.

(various Essex rectors); Manchester, John Rylands University Library, MS English 81 (Syon Monastery); New York, Columbia University Library, Plimpton Additional MS 3 (Cathedral Priory of the Holy Trinity in Norwich); Oxford, Bodleian Library, MSS Bodley 277 (London Charterhouse), Bodley 771 (Shrewsbury, Franciscan convent), and Rawlinson C. 258 (Dominican recluse, Church of St. John, Newcastle-upon-Tyne).

⁴⁹ London, British Library, Egerton MSS 617–618 (Henry IV's brother, Thomas of Woodstock) and Royal 1 C. VIII (Henry VII); Oxford, Bodleian Library, MS Bodley 277 (Henry VI); Tokyo, Takamiya collection, MS 219 (Henry Percy); and Wolfenbuttel, Herzog-August-Bibliothek, Cod. Guelf. Aug. A. 2 (Henry V's brother Thomas of Lancaster).

⁵⁰ Eton College, MS 24 (Sir John de Lisle, copied by his clerk at Woodhouse on the Isle of Wight); Manchester, John Rylands University Library, MS English 81 (Lady Anne Danvers); Oxford, Bodleian Library, MS Douce 240 (Sir Thomas Peverel); and Worcester, Worcester Cathedral Libary, MS F. 172 (Sir Thomas Cook).

⁵¹ For example, Manchester, John Rylands University Library, MS English 77 (a mother living in fifteenth-century London); Oxford, New College, MS 320 (William Huchen) or Bodleian Library, MS Douce 265 (Richard Hornby's mother). There are also a few copies with arms that remain unidentified, such as Cambridge, MA, Harvard University Library, Richardson MS 3.

⁵² London, British Library, MS Egerton 2880.

THE GENERAL PROLOGUE AS README.TXT

Despite the evident popularity of the Wycliffite Bible, the threat posed by Arundel and the potential for a shift toward proprietary control of parts of the information commons was clearly taken seriously in some quarters. What is today called the General Prologue was written by a Lollard who took part in the Wycliffite Bible's development, and though it is contained in only a few copies of the Wycliffite Bible, it forms the earliest recorded statement of hacker values.[53] Using rhetoric familiar to hackers today, the General Prologue's author claimed that the Bible was a commons and should therefore be both open in the vernacular and freely available. Rita Copeland claims that the Lollards desired to "releas[e] the *text* [of the Bible] from the imprisonment of mere language so that it [could] be a newly collective property," but I argue that there was nothing new about treating the Bible as an information commons: what was new was defending why one did so.[54] As a threat to a traditional information commons developed in the form of an anti-translation position promoted by the Church hierarchy and supported by the government, so too did a vocal response to that threat.

Readme files are theoretically written for a mixed audience, but practically speaking today they are read, if at all, only by other programmers. The README.TXT file includes general information about a program, including credits to

---

[53] The General Prologue exists today in only nine complete and partial copies of the Wycliffite Bible. See Dove, *First English Bible*, 1, and also Anne Hudson, *Selections from English Wycliffite Writings* (Cambridge, UK: Cambridge University Press, 1978), 67–72 and notes. For a more recently prepared edition, see *The Earliest Advocates of the English Bible: The Texts of the Medieval Debate*, ed. Mary Dove (Exeter: University of Exeter Press, 2010).

[54] Rita Copeland, "Toward a Social Genealogy of Translation Theory: Classical Property Law and Lollard Property Reform," in *Translation Theory and Practice in the Middle Ages,* ed. Jeanette Beer (Kalamazoo, MI: Medieval Institute Publications, 1997), 182 [173–183].

the developers and copyright information, as well as installation instructions. These files also include more specialized information used by programmers alone, such as the changelog, or record of changes made to the program since the last version, together with a list of known bugs.

Like a medieval readme file, the General Prologue of the Wycliffite Bible appears to be a sort of medieval version of modern developer release notes and FAQs, available for the "full release" of this particular open source project.[55] The General Prologue seems to have been written with a mixed audience in mind, just as readme files are today, and with similar contents. As such, it provides both basic instruction in biblical interpretation and, in Chapter 15, careful description of the methodology used by the team of translators. This is not quite a changelog, but it is close. As Hudson notes, the methodology described in this project description is deceptively simple: to have accomplished it would have required an enormous number of hours and a group of dedicated scholars.[56] In Chapter 15, the prologue author, calling himself "Simple Creature" (pseudonymity is an ancient hacker tradition) also outlines the reasons why the project was undertaken, and these emphasize the hacker ideals of commonness, openness, and freedom.[57]

---

[55] While "FAQ" has now entered the general lexicon, Raymond reminds us that it originated in hacker circles and referred specifically to frequently asked questions *about programming*: see Raymond, *Dictionary,* 181. Recently, Henry Ansgar Kelly has forwarded a persuasive argument that the text known as the General Prologue of the Wycliffite Bible was neither general nor a prologue, and that it was written by a Lollard who took only a small role in the development of the LV: Henry Ansgar Kelly, "The Middle English Bible: Hijacked by the Wycliffites?", conference paper, Annual Meeting of the Medieval Academy, Tempe, Arizona, April 14-16, 2011. I am grateful to Henry Kelly for providing this material to me.

[56] Anne Hudson, "Wyclif and the English Language," in *Wyclif in His Times,* ed. Anthony Kenny (Oxford: Clarendon, 1986), 92–93 [85–103].

[57] Copeland herself notices the importance of openness to the Wyc-

It should be noted how the General Prologue offered to provide another layer of accretion over the Wycliffite Bible, but its limited circulation did not create the necessary coverage for a new stratum. If we think of the Wycliffite Bible as a category killer that overshadowed other, partial translations, then it was a significant layer of cultural deposit. In contrast, the General Prologue's layer of accretion turned out to be far less widespread in the medieval period than the volume to which it was so seldom attached. Accretion this may have been, but it was localized only, and we must assume that few Wycliffite Bible owners read it. Most of us never open the developer or FAQ files on computer programs today, either. Nevertheless, it is worth considering this rare prologue because the author reminded his audience of the tradition of the Bible as an information commons at a time when institutional forces were attempting to exert control over that commons. These hacker sentiments might never have been voiced had it not been for the threat to that tradition posed by the Constitutions.

That Simple Creature was writing largely, though not exclusively, for other translators and editors, for other hackers, has not been credited before now. However, the Wycliffite Bible was an enormous, and therefore unusual, translation enterprise and its outlawing in 1409 rendered it even more special, particularly when its immediate popularity is considered. Much about Chapter 15 specifically might be of interest to other medieval hackers, as they could have had professional interest in the methods used in such a monumental task, together with professional curiosity about the reasons behind it. From the perspective of the early fifteenth-century, if the Church was attempting to restrain scripture translation, there was no way to know what else might be curtailed. In this sense Chapter 15 might also be viewed as a consciousness-raising gesture in an effort to begin to build a

---

liffite translational theory in *Pedagogy, Intellectuals, and Dissent in the Later Middle Ages* (Cambridge, UK: Cambridge University Press, 2001), 114.

coalition out of an educated, skilled community only very recently threatened.

The General Prologue claims to give readers an insight into the working practices of the Wycliffite Bible developers, and these parallel those of open source project teams today. The team that labored to bring the Wycliffite Bible into being may well have been a diverse group whose beliefs ran the gamut from orthodox to heretical: we have no way of knowing for sure. Moreover, this team developed the Wycliffite Bible in stages comparable to those of open source software. Further, as we have already seen, once released, the Wycliffite Bible was developed and reused in ways that the original developers might not have anticipated. Regardless, the popularity of the Wycliffite Bible is exactly what the Lollards declared should happen: the common text of the Bible should be open to the people in the vernacular and should move freely among the community of English people of whatever confession.

The General Prologue begins by arguing for the commonness of the scripture for all Christian communities: "because Christ says that the Gospel shall be preached throughout the whole world."[58] The Prologue continues by quoting (and translating) Jerome on Psalm 87: "Holy Writ is the scripture of the people for it was written so that all people should be familiar with it."[59] For the "common profit," translating the Bible is "common charity."[60] It was a common project: the Prologue calls the team "a variety of colleagues and assistants" who undertook each stage of the process, from gathering materials, to establishing a best Latin text, to seeking out additional expert linguistic advice, to making a pre-

---

[58] For the text of the General Prologue, see Hudson, *Selections*, 67–72. Hereafter, General Prologue quotations will be cited by line number. GP, 1: "for as myche as Crist seiþ þat þe gospel shal be prechid in al þe world."

[59] GP, 6–7: "holi writ is þe scripture of puplis for it is maad þat alle puplis shulden knowe it."

[60] GP, 24, 129: "comoun profyt," "comune charite."

liminary translation, to revision of that translation.[61] By including a plea to educated readers for revision of any faults, the author encouraged continued participation in this open source project.[62] This invitation to further revision was a commonplace in the medieval information commons, and it was a tradition eventually contested by the humanists, as we will see in Chapter 4.

Openness was a goal of the translation. The goal, stated in similar language several times, was to make the biblical sentence "as open or even more open in English than in Latin"[63] The Prologue goes on to give grammatical examples of "opening" Latin using English.[64] Jerome's standard of sense-translation lies at the heart of this open source project: "this will in many places make the meaning open, where to English it literally would render it dark and difficult."[65]

Openness is one of a group of terms that mark a so-called "Lollard vocabulary." It was closely linked to the Lollard program for lay access to the Bible and implied easy access through clarity of translation.[66] For Lollards, this openness related to unmediated access to the divine intention conveyed in scripture.[67] "Open" scripture is contrasted with

---

[61] GP, 27–35: "diuerse felawis and helperis."

[62] GP, 69–71.

[63] GP, 38: "as opin eiþer openere in English as in Latyn." See also GP, 67–69: "I purposide wiþ Goddis helpe to make þe sentence as trewe and open in English as it is in Latyn, eiþer more trewe and more open þan it is in Latyn," and again at 85 and 90.

[64] Copeland herself uses "opening" to describe this process in "Genealogy," 179.

[65] GP, 55–56: "þis wole in manie placis make þe sentence open, where to englisshe it aftir þe word wolde be derk and doutful." For discussion of Jerome's understanding of sense translation, see Rita Copeland, *Rhetoric, Hermeneutics, and Translation in The Middle Ages: Academic Traditions and Vernacular Texts* (Cambridge, UK: Cambridge University Press, 1995), 43–53, generally.

[66] Nicole Rice, *Lay Piety and Religious Discipline in Middle English Literature* (Cambridge, UK: Cambridge University Press, 2008), 70.

[67] Kantik Ghosh, *Wycliffite Heresy: Authority and the Interpretation of Texts* (Cambridge, UK: Cambridge University Press, 2002), 160.

"dark" scripture, but Lollards insisted that clerical mediation was not necessary to comprehend scripture in either case, for those in charity. Nevertheless, Nicole Rice has shown that "openness" was a popular adjective in non-Lollard circles as well. In these uses clergy might still assist in mediating between "dark" scripture and "open," and the sense of accessibility stands behind either interpretation.[68] As I said in Chapter 1, "openness" continues to refer to access even today, though the nuances involved in that access may change over time.

Freedom is addressed too, as this translation must be envisioned to circulate freely in order "to save all men in our realm whom God wishes to be saved."[69] The Prologue accuses the clergy of closing, of limiting, access to scripture when they "prevent Holy Writ from circulating as much as they may."[70] Freedom is also implicit in the Prologue's list of other translations of the Bible. First written in Hebrew and Greek, the Bible was translated into vernacular Latin, had in the past been translated into Old English, and was currently available in several Continental vernaculars. Why, the author asks, are others free to access the Bible in their own languages, but anglophones alone are left without scripture in the common tongue?[71] The author of the General Prologue implies that the Bible should be freely available.

Because of the existence of the medieval information commons, I disagree with Mary Dove's belief that "EV was never intended to be copied as a translation in its own right, but that translators producing the LV lost control of what happened to the EV in the early 1380s."[72] In the 1370s the

---

[68] Rice, *Lay Piety*, 71–72.
[69] GP, 24–25: "to saue alle men in oure rewme whiche God wole haue sauid."
[70] GP, 22: "stoppen holi writ as myche as þei moun." I believe that "stoppen" here has the sense of a stopper preventing liquid from flowing, so the sense of artificially prevented circulation is original to the Middle English text.
[71] GP, 131–172.
[72] Dove, *First English Bible*, 3.

Wycliffite Bible project was part of a tradition of treating the Bible as an information commons. Indeed, the Wycliffite Bible may have been one culmination of that tradition. The EV and the LV were both produced to be copied, to become part of the information commons in their turn. Without more information I do not think we can assume the collaborators wanted to control either EV or LV. The Bible in Middle English attracted interest from many quarters in the following decades and the tradition of bible translation eventually came to be questioned. In an era increasingly willing to condone institutional control (however imperfect) over texts, the author of the General Prologue emphatically expressed the significance of treating the Bible as an information commons.

By the time Lydgate was translating the psalms in the fifteenth century, hacking biblical text into Middle English had over one hundred years of tradition behind it. Like the hacked statutes in Chapter 2, we must assume that much of the audience for these texts knew exactly what they were reading. The linguistic landscape of fifteenth-century England was too complex for us to assume that these English texts served only as glosses to Latin texts, any more than hacked statutes were simple cribs. Glosses they may have been, sometimes and for some people, but clearly these texts also stood on their own and served as their traditional counterparts. The Bible was a traditional information commons, and the Wycliffite hackers like the author of the General Prologue voiced strong opposition to Arundel's effort at containment. More effective than the manifesto in the General Prologue, however, was the product of that production team's labors, the Wycliffite Bible, which spread freely across England and was developed further throughout the century.

In this chapter we see the beginning of the changes that transform the textual world in the sixteenth century, and that continue to inform textual culture today. In the fifteenth century attempts at controlling the information commons remained local and imperfect, and they failed to effectively sediment a new textual order. However, the local accretions gradually grew together. Approached from a modernist, or even an Early Modernist perspective, the century between Thomas Arundel and Thomas More may seem long, and the lives of the two men entirely unconnected. However, when perceived from the other vantage, one can see unspooling behind both men the hundreds of years during which the culture of the information commons had permeated society. From that perspective such an enormous change taking a mere century to develop momentum seems swift indeed.

Chapter 4: Tyndale and the Joye of Piracy[1]

The defensive statement of hacker values in the Wycliffite Bible General Prologue turned out to be unnecessary. The Wycliffite Bible continued to surface as the main English biblical translation through the early sixteenth century, and overlaps in use with a new group of English biblical translations being produced by self-conscious hackers, some of whom were influenced methodologically by humanism. While the Wycliffites had been content to hack the Latin

---

[1] While we will consider George Joye as a hacker later, Julia Child understood herself to be opening a proprietary set of practices (the art of cooking) that she believed to be common, and by writing the *Joy of Cooking* she helped those practices to freely circulate. Raymond also plays on the "joy of x" formula in a subsection-title: Eric S. Raymond, *The Cathedral and the Bazaar: Musings on Linux and Open Source by an Accidental Revolutionary* (New York: O'Reilly, 1999), 100.

Vulgate (if carefully compiling a best-text before doing so), the sixteenth-century translators were informed by humanist methods of textual scholarship. They labored to master the biblical languages of Hebrew and Greek (and eventually Aramaic), and made use of the best humanist editions and translations available. Thanks in large part to his linguistic facility, William Tyndale overshadowed other early sixteenth-century English bible translators. As we will see in this chapter, Tyndale was unique in other ways as well, and broke from medieval tradition in the intellectual property claims he made over his translations. The tradition of bible hacking that we saw in Chapter 3 persisted into the 1530s before being brought under Tudor control, and Tyndale's death as a martyr led his translations to become part of the base code Miles Coverdale used when compiling the authorized 1539/40 Great Bible, whether Tyndale wished it or not. Tyndale's translations and the Great Bible together laid down new cultural strata of enormous significance.

Like two geologic plates sliding past each other while each undergoes its own gradual sedimentation, I trace twin developments in this chapter, each made up of smaller, individual practices. The information commons was stressed by several sets of forces that together restricted the commons. Individually none of these forces could have effected this change, but together that is precisely what occurred. First, as Tyndale's behavior shows, humanism was changing the culture of authorship. Second, Henry VIII's censorship was not all-powerful, as Tyndale's textual career attests. Yet, once that autocratic ruler supported bible translation, the powerful state censorship machine could gain enough support from bible hackers themselves to succeed. This last point illustrates the importance of the cooperation of the hacker community with institutional forces. Only when some hackers came to work for the king could the commons be limited. Seismic activity occurs at any transform boundary, as plates slide past each other, troubling the landscape above. The 1530s and 1540s experienced a very troubled landscape, indeed.

Unlike the Wycliffite Bible's theoretically straightforward (if ineffective) illegality born in 1409, the sixteenth century witnessed a complicated progression of book bans, authorizations, and privileges that labored to effectively channelize religious writing. The 1409 Constitutions were still in effect, as was *De heretico comburendo*, the law that empowered the state to burn heretics. This licensed the government to take steps, but as the failure to stop the Wycliffite Bible in the fifteenth century demonstrated, more regulation was needed to truly control textual production.[2] As they had in the fifteenth century, the ecclesiastical hierarchy took a leading role. Lutheran texts appear to have made their way to England by the 1520s, and already in 1521, Cardinal Wolsey was collecting, condemning, and burning Lutheran books. After 1529 royal proclamations including lists of banned books were common. A proclamation in 1538 finalized the need for every text being published in England to be reviewed by a royally approved inspector. We shall see by the end of this chapter how the eventual authorization of an English bible by the king, now head of the English Church, put a significant throttle on the open development characteristic of earlier periods.

While Tyndale's work was absolutely crucial, the bible hacking in these years was complex, rather than simple, and the varied results of this hacking bear consideration as interrelated cultural productions. James Andrew Clark notes that "sixteenth-century Bible translators differed from their secu-

---

[2] The bibliography on early Tudor censorship is vast, but for the short, classic account, see A.W. Pollard, "The Regulation of the Book Trade in the Sixteenth Century," *The Library*, 3rd series, 7 (1916): 18–43, and W.W. Greg's response to this piece in "*Ad Imprimendum Solum*," *The Library*, 3rd series, 9 (1954): 242–247. Greg's disagreement with Pollard on the interpretation of the 1538 proclamation does not concern us in this chapter. See also John B. Gleason, "The Earliest Evidence for Ecclesiastical Censorship of Printed Books in England," *The Library* 4 (1982): 135–141, and D. M. Loades, "The Press Under the Early Tudors: A Study in Censorship and Sedition," *Transactions of the Cambridge Bibliographical Society* 4 (1968): 29–50.

lar counterparts in their emphasis on slow and steady progress achieved by a multiple of hands . . . trying out alternate readings."[3] He includes Luther in this very open source-style description, and contrasts Tyndale, who worked noticeably alone. In this chapter we will concentrate on a few of the many hackers who translated the Bible as a common text they planned to open into English and make free. However, for the first time we see a hacker claim some property rights over his translation. For Tyndale, the Bible should be common, open, and free, but only if he had control over what was done to it after its release. No other sixteenth-century biblehacker made this claim, and we will examine Tyndale's claims and the hacker community's response to them in detail below. Tyndale's property claims mark a fundamental shift away from the information commons we have traced until now, and point toward the enclosure of the Bible as semi-proprietary in the 1540s. That intellectual property took another two hundred years to crystallize into law should remind us of how remarkable Tyndale's position was, and how forcefully information commons asserted themselves, even after privileges and patents began to corral them.

Like the Wycliffite Bible translators before them, these early evangelical hackers argued that the Bible was common, and therefore should be open and free. Time and again we will see them express in prefaces and prologues that the Bible is a text common to all English people. As a common text the Bible should therefore be open, accessible in the common tongue. Further, the prefaces we will consider speak of translating as opening scripture, and making it light where it was dark.[4] Finally, as a common text, the English Bible should be

---

[3] James Andrew Clark, "Norm and License in Tyndale's New Testament Translation," *William Tyndale and the Law,* eds. John A.R. Dick and Anne Richard (Kirksville, MO: Sixteenth Century Journal Publishers, 1994), 62–63 [59–68].

[4] On this trope as important to later reformers, see John King, "'The Light of Printing,' William Tyndale, John Foxe, John Day, and Early Modern Print Culture," *Renaissance Quarterly* 54 (2001): 52–85.

free, circulating among all levels of English society, from Henry VIII to the plowman invoked by Luther and Tyndale.

In this chapter we address in detail an early historical instance of what scholars too often call intellectual piracy: George Joye's contentious 1534 revision of Tyndale's 1526 New Testament. The term "piracy" is usually applied uncritically.[5] When Tyndale claimed that Joye had corrupted his text, Joye argued instead that he was merely editing and correcting a poor copytext. The incident highlights the differing notions of intellectual property held by the two men. I argue that Tyndale's claims to intellectual property are exceptional and that, in contrast, Joye's approach features a traditional understanding of the Bible as part of the information commons that we have traced from the beginning of this book. Scholars confuse the issues when they use terms inappropriately. Tyndale's biographer David Daniell is exempletive; he cautions that copyright is a very modern and contested notion, and then proceeds to use "piracy" throughout an article without further exploration of the term.[6] Recently, Gergely Jushász follows the leads of Joye's biographers, Butterworth and Chester, and points out that to use a term like "piracy" as we mean it today with regard to copyright is anachronistic.[7]

---

[5] Along with the examples I will discuss below, Charles Nesbitt also uses the term: "Mercenary Motives in the Production of the English Bible in the Early Sixteenth Century," *Anglican Theological Review* 34 (1952): 158 [154–166]. Orlaith O'Sullivan makes a related error, assuming a translator was responsible for selecting the decoration of a particular work: "The Bible Translations of George Joye," in *The Bible as Book: The Reformation,* ed. Orlaith O'Sullivan (London: The British Library, 2000), 26 [25–38].

[6] David Daniell, "Tyndale, Roye, Joye, and Copyright," in *William Tyndale and the Law,* eds. John A.R. Dick and Anne Richardson (Kirksville, MO: Sixteenth Century Journal Publishers, 1994), 93–101.

[7] Gergely Jushász, "Some Neglected Aspects of the Exegetical Debate on Resurrection and the Immortality of the Soul between William Tyndale and George Joye in Antwerp (1534-1535)," *Reformation* 14 (2009): 21 [1–47].

Nevertheless, Butterworth and Chester make free use of the term "unauthorized" instead, which is also problematic, since one faces logical difficulties when considering authorized and unauthorized editions of banned books.[8]

Butterworth and Chester claim that "no one could claim the author's rights in the Word of God, and as yet the question of the rights of the translator had not been raised," but I will argue below that Tyndale raises precisely those questions. I argue further that he suggests radically that a translator might own a text.[9] If Tyndale had not proposed it, the modern concept of plagiarism would not seem so apt to Andrew Hope in describing any biblical version based on Tyndale's work.[10] Recently, Meraud Grant Ferguson offers an exciting preliminary examination of printing privileges and contracts being used to protect intellectual property rights in England as early as 1510. Change was in the air, but Ferguson notes that outside of law printing such instruments did not become standard until much later.[11] Enclosing the infor-

---

[8] For example, see Charles Butterworth and Allan Chester, *George Joye 1495?-1553: A Chapter in the History of the English Bible and the English Reformation* (Philadelphia: University of Pennsylvania Press, 1962), 147 and following.

[9] Butterworth and Chester, *George Joye,* 165. James Simpson notes that "the text is now the property not of its readers and interpreters, but rather of its translator," but he is not addressing intellectual property issues particularly in his argument in *Burning to Read: English Fundamentalism and its Reformation Opponents* (Cambridge, MA: The Belknap Press, 2007), 179.

[10] Andrew Hope, "Plagiarizing the Word of God: Tyndale between More and Joye," in *Plagiarism in Early Modern England,* ed. Paulina Kewes (New York: Palgrave, 2003), 93–105.

[11] Meraud Grant Ferguson, "'In Recompense of His Labours and Inuencyon': Early Sixteenth-Century Book Trade Privileges and the Birth of Literary Property in England," *Transactions of the Cambridge Bibliographical Society* 13 (2004): 14–32. For an unusual examination of early printing privileges, see Elizabeth Armstrong, *Before Copyright: The French Book-Privilege System 1498-1526* (Cambridge, UK: Cambridge University Press, 1990). Her introduction includes some discussion of privileges across Europe. For licenses in

mation commons remained a radical notion. Commons are bounded by custom, as we saw in Chapter 1, and I will argue that while Joye fully participates in customary handling of scripture, Tyndale is altogether confident that he has rights to his translation. As do modern scholars, Tyndale may well have viewed Joye as a pirate, but only because Tyndale's own insistence on his rights to his translation was pushing the boundaries of traditional culture. The persistent scholarly reminders of the term piracy's anachronism are a testament to the way in which history developed in Tyndale's footsteps, rather than along the customary paths tread by Joye.

IN THE CATHEDRAL: TYNDALE

Because our culture takes intellectual property for granted, because it is normative for us, I will begin with the historical exception, Tyndale. When hacker ethnographer Eric Raymond discusses proprietary computer code development, he uses the analogy of the cathedral. He says that large projects "needed to be built like cathedrals, carefully crafted by individual [experts] working in splendid isolation, with no beta released before its time."[12] Raymond's miraculously independent cathedral-builders are crafting an enormous complex edifice, so perfect that it can be a house of God, and they do not share how they accomplish this herculean task with others. Moreover, while not everyone can build a cathedral, countless numbers will enter one.

In translating the New Testament and parts of the Old Testament, Tyndale was building a textual cathedral. While insisting that scripture be common, open, and free, Tyndale also attempted to enforce his rights to his translations, an action contrary to the traditional information commons.[13]

---

the Netherlands specifically, see Prosper Verheyden, "Drukkersoctrooien in de 16e Eeuw," *Tijd-schrift voor Boek-en Bibliotheekswezen* 8 (1910): 202–278.

[12] Raymond, *The Cathedral and the Bazaar,* 29.

[13] Raymond, *The Cathedral and the Bazaar,* 82–83. The "cathedral"

The necessity of scripture being open to the faithful by being translated into the common tongue is a prevalent theme throughout early evangelical writing. In his prologue to his exposition on Matthew, Tyndale uses the analogy of removing a veil to describe the opening of scripture into the vernacular.[14] Yet in his prologue to the *Exposition of the First Epistle of Saint John*, Tyndale notes that translation into the "common tongue" is not sufficient, but it must also be light, so that it is "an open preaching."[15] In his preface to the Pentateuch, Tyndale lays out his position most succinctly: "This thing alone moved me to translate the New Testament: experience had taught me how impossible it was to teach truth to laypeople unless the scripture was plainly laid before their eyes in the mother tongue."[16] In the first preface to his 1534

---

and the "bazaar" are not mutually exclusive. In fact, Raymond associates the more pragmatic, market-friendly forces in the open source community with Linux founder Linus Torvalds, and contrasts them with the followers of strict open source-proponent Richard Stallman: Raymond, *Cathedral and the Bazaar*, 85–86. Clark notices the contrast between Tyndale's solitary working and the traditional "idealized images of collective labor" normal in scriptural translation efforts in "Norm and License," 63.

[14] William Tyndale, *An exposicion vppon the. v. vi. vii. chapters of Mathew* [Antwerp?: de Keyser, 1533?], STC 24440, fol. A2r. ESTC lists this printer as possibly Grapheus, but Paul Valkema-Blouw argues convincingly that most of the questionable imprints are de Keyser's: "Early Modern Protestant Publications in Antwerp, 1526-30: The Pseudonymous Adam Anonymous and Hans Luft of Marlborow," *Quaerendo* 26 (1996): 94–110.

[15] William Tyndale, *The exposition of the fyrste epistle of seynt Jhon with a prologge before it* [Antwerp: Marten de Keyser], 1531, STC 24443, fols. A7r-v, "an open preaching." In the quotations from Early Modern English included in this chapter, I am silently expanding abbreviations, minimizing special characters, and regularizing u/v for readability in the notes. In the text I use my own modernization.

[16] William Tyndale, [The Pentateuch] [Antwerp: de Keyser, 1530], STC 2350, fol. [A]2v, "Which thinge onlye moved me to translate the new testament. Because I had perceaved by experyence / how

revised New Testament, Tyndale asserts that his marginal glosses and commentaries provide a "a true key with which to open [scripture]."[17]

As the hackers say, Tyndale had an itch to scratch, the need for an English bible, and in the early 1520s, he began working with pre-existing code, Erasmus' 1522 Greek-Latin New Testament (and later Erasmian Hebrew Old Testaments), in order to develop a solution.[18] Tyndale's 1525/6 New Testament was his first attempt at solving the problem of an English New Testament, and it was admittedly imperfect; as Raymond puts it, "you often don't really understand the problem until after the first time you implement a solution."[19] The eventual complete printing of Tyndale's New

---

that it was impossible to stablysh the laye people in any truth/ excepte the scripture were playnly layde before their eyes in their mother tonge."

[17] William Tyndale, *The newe Testament, dylygently corrected and compared with the Greke by Willyam Tindale* [Antwerp: Marten Emperowr, 1534], STC 2826, fol. *2v, "true keye to open [scripture] with all." Hereafter in the notes this edition is designated as T1534.

[18] Raymond, *The Cathedral and the Bazaar*, 32–34, 57, and Juhász, 272n1384. See also Gergely Juhász, "The Bible and the Early Reformation Period," in *Tyndale's Testament*, eds. Paul Arblaster, Gergely Juhász and Guido Latré (Turnhout: Brepols, 2002), 27, and Gilbert Tournoy, "*Testamentum Novum* (Basel, Johann Froben, July 1522)," in *Tyndale's Testament*, eds. Paul Arblaster, Gergely Juhász and Guido Latré (Turnhout: Brepols, 2002), 88–89.

[19] Raymond, *The Cathedral and the Bazaar*, 35. See also Gergely M. Jushász, *Translating Resurrection: An Early Sixteenth-Century Exegetical Debate in Antwerp Between the Protestant Bible Translators William Tyndale and George Joye and its Historical and Theological Context*, Ph.D. diss., Katholieke Universiteit Leuven, 2008, 272n1387, and Gergely M. Jushász, *Translating Resurrection: The Debate Between William Tyndale and George Joye and Its Historical and Theological Context* (Leiden: Brill, 2014). I would like to thank Dr. Juhász for sharing his thesis with me in advance of its publication. Juhász, "Neglected," 3. Even Tyndale's source text was imperfect, being based on late manuscripts, and not entirely transparent. Erasmus' text shows that he sometimes translated the Greek from the Latin. For bibliography about Erasmus' back-translations, see

Testament in Worms in 1526 contains only a short epilogue to the reader, and admits "the rudeness of the work," due in part to it being a first effort, "a thing not having its full shape, but like something born prematurely, something begun, but not yet completed."[20]

At least in theory, Tyndale also adhered to Raymond's dictum that "treating your users as co-developers is your least-hassle route to rapid code improvement and effective debugging," as when Tyndale admitted the imperfections of his text, initially he requested assistance in revision.[21] Tyndale's first attempt at printing his translation in 1525 was famously foiled, and the remaining "Cologne fragments" circulated such as they were.[22] In the extant Cologne fragment, the translator makes the following request: "if they perceive any places where I have not achieved the precise sense of the language or scriptural meaning or have not used the right English word that they amend it themselves, remembering that it is their duty to do so."[23] This call for revi-

---

Juhász, *Translating Resurrection*, 272n1387. Erasmus revised his text persistently, finding it acceptable only after five editions; see Tournoy, "*Testmentum Novum*," 88–89.

[20] William Tyndale, [*The newe Testame[n]t, as it was written and caused to be writte[n] by them which herde yt*] [Worms: Peter Schöffer?, 1526?], STC 2824, fol. 344v, "the rudenes off the worke," "a thynge not havynge his full shape, but as it were borne afore hys tyme, even as a thing begunne rather than fynnesshed." See the facsimile in W.R. Cooper, ed., *The New Testament. Translated by William Tyndale: The Text of the Worms Edition of 1526 in the Original Spelling* (London: The British Library, 2000). Hereafter this edition will be cited as T1526.

[21] Raymond, *The Cathedral and the Bazaar*, 37.

[22] For this story see David Daniell, *William Tyndale: A Biography* (New Haven: Yale University Press, 1994), 108–133.

[23] William Tyndale, [*The New Testament*] [Cologne: Peter Quentell?, 1525], STC 2823, fol. A2r, "yf they perceyve in 'eny places that y have not attayned the very sence of the tonge/ or meanynge of the scripture/ or have not geven the right englysshe word/ that they put to there hands to amende it/ remembrynge that so is there duetie to doo." Hereafter this edition will be cited as T1525.

sions, for debugging, is echoed in most printed bible prefaces before the Great Bible, and as we shall see in the next chapter, also in the early printed translated statute collections. Moreover, these pleas are far from being simply holdovers from medieval modesty topos, as hackers utilize each others' work today and did in the Middle Ages too.[24]

But Tyndale did not follow through on these nods to open source development, and increasingly limited his pool of acceptable co-developers. While in his 1525 preface he says he will "release early, release often," to take advantage of suggested revisions, by 1526 he says instead "in time to come . . . we will give it his full shape."[25] That is, Tyndale himself would revise Tyndale's own work, and he continues to place limitations on whom he gives the rights of revision after 1526. In his preface to the Pentateuch of 1530, Tyndale grants only those knowing Hebrew with the right to revise his work: he "submit[s] this book and all the rest that I have written or translated or will in the future . . . to be corrected by them, banned, and even burned if it seems worthwhile after they have compared it with the Hebrew text, as long as they first publish their own, more correct translation."[26] These are strong words. By the fall of 1534, Tyndale had turned

---

[24] For just a sample of scholarly discussion on the medieval dullness-trope, see David Lawton, "Dullness and the Fifteenth Century," *ELH* 54 (1987): 761–799, and Seth Lerer, *Chaucer and His Readers: Imagining the Author in Late-Medieval England* (Princeton: Princeton University Press, 1993), 4, where he notes memorably that "in their own, equally effusive protestations of incompetence or dullness, the writers of the century appear to make a poetry so bad that it is virtually unreadable."

[25] T1526, fol. 344v. Tyndale continues with a list of issues he intends to address in a subsequent, improved edition. See Raymond, *The Cathedral and the Bazaar*, 39.

[26] Tyndale, [*The Pentateuch*], fol. [A]4v, "submytte[s] this boke and all other that I have other made or translated/ or shall in tyme to come . . . to be corrected of them/ yee and moreover to be disalewed & also burnte/ if it seme worthy when they have examyned it wyth the hebrue/ so that they first put forth of their awne translatinge a nother that is more correcte."

back to the New Testament, and produced a substantial revision. His comments about editing the New Testament call to mind those of the earlier Pentateuch preface: "If anyone finds fault either with the translation or otherwise (which is easier for many to do than to have translated it themselves with their own intellects . . .) they can translate it themselves and put whatever they want into it. If I find myself or thanks to the help of others that any mistake has been made or might be translated more plainly then I will have it fixed quickly."[27] The barriers to entry here are steep; only reading the original languages *and* producing an entirely new, unique translation are sufficient. As critic James Simpson notes tartly: "this isn't anyone's idea of the opening paragraph of an open Bible."[28]

---

[27] T1534, fols.1v–2r, "If anye man fynde fautes ether with the translacion or ought besyde (which is easyer for manye to do then so well to have translated it them selves of their awne pregnant wyttes . . .) to the same it shal be law full to translate it them selves and to put what they lust therto. If I shall perceave ether by my selfe or by the informacion of other/ that ought be escaped me/ or myght be more playnlye translated/ I will shortlye after cause it to be mended."

[28] Simpson, *Burning to Read*, 178. Simpson suggests that Tyndale offers relatively free revision in *Parable of the Wicked Mammon,* where Tyndale says "to all men, to correct it, whosoever could" (Simpson, *Burning to Read,* 177). I disagree: the context of the quotation he offers suggests less correction, than it does an all-or-none attitude toward his audience:

> Nevertheless in translatinge the new testamente I did my dutye/ and so doo I now/ and will doo as moch more as god hath ordened me to doo. And as I offered that to all men to correcte it/ whoso ever coulde even so doo I this Who so ever therefore readest thys/ compare it unto the scripture. If gods worde beare recorde unto it and thous also felest in thine herte that it is so be of good comfort and geve god thankes. Iff gods worde condemne it/ then hold it acursyd/ and so do all other doctrines.

For Tyndale in the *Parable*, his audience will either find his work synchronous with the scripture in their hearts or they will not and so will reject the *Parable* utterly. Further, in the *Parable,* Tyndale's

Raymond cautions that "the next best thing to having good ideas is recognizing good ideas from your users. Sometimes the latter is better."[29] Yet it is clear that over time Tyndale continuously raised the bar in order to silence possible critics of his translation. Significantly, when Tyndale's corrected Pentateuch was reissued in 1534 with a new preface even his limited request for revision was lacking, suggesting that Joye's revisions of the 1526 New Testament appeared when Tyndale's willingness to accept revision, already wavering, was at a particularly low ebb.[30]

Tyndale's anger at nonauthorial revision was a variation on a growing tradition of frustration with printers, one in which Erasmus and Luther took part as well. David McKitterick uses Erasmus' comments about the variety in print quality as an extended illustration of how early print authors saw these issues. McKitterick notes that "he saw in his printers, Aldus Manutius in Venice and Froben in Basel, examples of responsibility to ancient texts that he found wholly admirable" and contrasts them with what Erasmus called "those common printers who reckon one pitiful gold coin in the way of profit worth more than the whole realm of letters."[31] Later, Erasmus expressed concern at the lack of quality control in the printing industry, a lack that contrasted sharply with the (at least theoretical) controls over most handicrafts.[32] In the end, Erasmus was arguing against "printers eager for easy

---

reference to his revision offer for his 1526 New Testament is disingenuous, as we have seen above (Simpson, *Burning,* 177): William Tyndale, [*Parable of the wicked mammon*] [Antwerp, 1528], STC 24454, fol. A5r.

[29] Raymond, *The Cathedral and the Bazaar,* 48.

[30] William Tyndale, *The first boke of Moses called Genesis newly correctyd and amendyd by W.T.* (Antwerp: de Keyser, 1534), STC 2351.

[31] David McKitterick, *Print, Manuscript, and the Search for Order, 1450-1830* (Cambridge, UK: Cambridge University Press, 2003), 109.

[32] McKitterick, *Search for Order,* 110.

profit or who cared nothing for their responsibilities either to the texts that they printed or to their markets."[33]

Martin Luther threw fits over intellectual property that provide specific examples of Erasmus' frustration. In several monitory prefaces Luther lashes out at shoddy printing.[34] In a postille of the 1520s, he calls unscrupulous printers "highwaymen and thieves." Particularly galling to Luther was that at least one of these pirate printings was made from an imperfect, unfinished copy that had been stolen by a typesetter, or so he claimed. Like Erasmus, Luther is concerned about the print quality of these hasty productions: they "hurry so much that I do not recognize my own books when they come back to me. There something is left out, there something is set wrong, there falsified, there not corrected." Further, Luther accuses these printers of false advertising, and claims that such underhandedness misleads a less-educated audience: "they print 'Wittemberg' in front of all sorts of books, which were neither made nor have been in Wittemberg. These are boys' pranks, to betray the common man." Such practices "betray people under our name." Such worries recall those of the preface to Rolle's *English Psalter* discussed in Chapter 3. In a fascinating insight into printing practices, Luther admits that proofing of his own holograph is necessary, so that stealing even Luther's own copy does not free a pirate printer's edition from error. Unlike Tyndale, Luther appears to welcome open source practice, at least to a degree, offering his holograph to anyone who wants to "improve and correct it." The preface was directed not only at the most recently piratical printer, but to all printers, and Luther demands sternly that a printer "out of Christian love" should wait a month or two before copying another printer's work. Even into the 1540s, Luther was beating the same drum: "Avarice now strikes / and plays this knavish trick on our print-

---

[33] McKitterick, *Search for Order,* 111.

[34] M. Friedrich Franke, ed., *D. Martin Luther's* Kirchenpostille, Vol. 11 (Leipzig: Gebauersche Buchhandlung E. Schimmel, 1846), 15–16. My thanks to Jennifer Welsh for the translation of this postille.

ers/ whereby others are instantly reprinting [our translation] / and are thus depriving us of our work/ and expenses to their profit, / which is a downright public robbery."[35] In this later piece he calls such printers "rapacious pirate printers." In both the 1540s and the 1520s Luther attempted to educate audiences about piracy and the quality differences between a pirated and an "authorized" copy. Here is not only the vocabulary of manuscript production applied to printing, but also the humanist desire for best-practices. Further, Luther's screeds offer clear evidence of a developing cultural stratum separating sixteenth-century culture from the information commons characterizing the medieval past.

Like Tyndale in 1534, Luther expresses concern over what he calls piracy: theft and redistribution of what he views as his own property. Like Tyndale, Luther is concerned with the quality of the final products. If Luther's own corrections have not been made, and if he had not completed a manuscript, then one could not even pretend it was Luther's work as he had intended it to appear. Nevertheless, Luther was a hacker too, and he signals his desire for free development with his insistence that he will provide his own copy, a sort of "best text" to anyone who wants it for correcting and improving.[36] By the 1530s, Tyndale had no interest in such open policies.

The contrast between the two arguments is significant. Luther rails at printers, not at editors as does Tyndale. Luther recognizes who is making the money on this piracy, directs his ire there, and goes further in offering a no-cost, quality alternative. Tyndale's decision to castigate Joye makes very little pragmatic sense if his genuine goal was to halt hacking of his work. That Tyndale took the unique step of attacking an editor, rather than the printers, marks the degree to which

---

[35] Luther's "Warning to the Printers" (1545), trans. Luis Sundkvist, in *Primary Sources on Copyright (1450-1900)*, eds. L. Bently & M. Kretschmer, www.copyrighthistory.org.

[36] Luther appears to have welcomed community assistance in his translations, as his well-known weekly meeting with his 'Sanhedrin' attests. See Heiko Oberman, *Luther: Man Between God and the Devil* (New Haven: Yale University Press, 2006), 308.

he saw his translation as property, and shows his understanding of his own reputation and power within the evangelical community. Hope argues that publishing costs were often split three ways, and that the author might be responsible for one of those shares.[37] Yet the copyeditors of printing houses often served as small-time translators and editors, and their pay was clearly not high. Given Joye's exceptionally poor remuneration for his editing he cannot have been part of financing the "pirate" editions.[38] It is precisely because of the finances involved that Tyndale could not succeed against the printers. He could only attack Joye, a fellow hacker.

IN THE BAZAAR, OR CAMMERSTRAAT: JOYE

Raymond contrasts the proprietary cathedral-style of development with that of the bazaar, characterized by "release early and often, delegate everything you can, be open to the point of promiscuity."[39] Despite the term bazaar's associations with colonialism, it is clear that what Raymond means is a particularly open and free type of marketplace. For practical purposes we can map the premodern urban market over Raymond's 'bazaar' quite easily (hence my subtitle's use of 'Cammerstraat,' a marketplace in Early Modern Antwerp). We have seen in the previous chapter how the Wycliffite translators released an imperfect beta version of their translation, how it attracted revisions from other hackers, and how it was finally released in a much-improved complete version that was also hacked by later editors. While Tyndale claimed to be doing this, Joye and Coverdale, among others, all actu-

---

[37] Andrew Hope, "On the Smuggling of Prohibited Books from Antwerp to England in the 1520s and 1530s," in *Tyndale's Testament,* eds. Paul Arblaster, Gergely Juhász and Guido Latré (Turnhout: Brepols, 2002), 35–38.

[38] See Guido Latré, "The 1535 Coverdale Bible and Its Antwerp Origins," in *The Bible as Book: The Reformation*, ed. Orlaith O'Sullivan (The British Library: London, 2000), 90–91 [89–102], for the work of copyeditors; see Juhász, "Neglected," 9n30, for Joye's payscale.

[39] Raymond, *The Cathedral and the Bazaar*, 30.

ally participated in such efforts. Like the Wycliffite Bible translators, they were the self-selected contributors to this particular development project.[40]

By the time he edited Tyndale's 1526 New Testament in 1534, Joye had developed a reputation as a scripture translator, primarily by working with the Old Testament and the psalms. Educated at Cambridge and partial to the reforms of Huldrych Zwingli, Joye worked as a copyeditor in Antwerp during his several periods of exile from England. His reputation was high enough among the English Nation in Antwerp to have become known in official circles as well. When Henry Phillips was given commissions to arrest three evangelicals in Antwerp in 1535, Tyndale alone was caught, but Joye's name was also on the list.[41] This is important to consider as we explore his dispute with Tyndale. Given that reputation among other hackers is a key motivator in hacker culture, Joye had something to lose and Tyndale knew it.[42]

Unlike Tyndale, Joye supported the notion that no single translation could be sufficient. As far back as 1531, the year of his first existing publications, Joye was calling for revisions to faulty scriptural translations, and highlighted in his "Prologue into the Prophet Isaiah," his plea to "burn no more God's word, but mend it where it is not translated correctly."[43] Unlike Tyndale's request for revision in 1525, Joye's appears to be sincere, and hinges on his open translation theory. Jushász says that Joye employed a "target language-oriented translation," and thus was exceptionally aware of how texts changed meaning in various cultural contexts. Following such a theory, no one translation can ever be sufficient.[44] Translating with an eye toward cultural context al-

---

[40] Raymond, *The Cathedral and the Bazaar*, 42.
[41] Butterworth and Chester, *George Joye,* 194–195.
[42] For the importance of reputation in hacker communities, see Coleman, generally, and especially Chapter 3.
[43] George Joye, *The prophete Isaye, translated into englysshe, by George Ioye* [Antwerp: de Keyser, 1531], STC 2777, fol. A4v, "burn nomore goddis worde: but mende it where it is not truly translated."
[44] Jushász, "Neglected," 32–33, 40.

lowed Joye to avoid directive notes to his readers and concentrate on *sola scriptura:* "Joye's inclination to variations in the translations is thus part and parcel of his universal translational strategy according to which he tries to render the original text in such a way that it does not necessitate any further explanations, remarks, marginal notes or other reading aids."[45] For Joye, a truly open text required no apparatus: "I wish that scripture was so purely and plainly translated that it required neither note, gloss, nor commentary so that the reader might swim without a float."[46] The contrast between Tyndale and Joye on this point is strong: "Tyndale's preference is for marginal glosses and the preservation of a stable text, [while] Joye's preference is for simply making the

---

[45] Jushász, *Translating,* 396. Hobbs notes that this translation strategy elaborates on that of Martin Bucer, which itself pushed Luther's methodologies to their limits: Gerald Hobbs, "Martin Bucer and the Englishing of the Psalms: Pseudonymity in the Service of Early English Protestant Piety," in *Martin Bucer: Reforming Church and Community,* ed. D. F. Wright (Cambridge, UK: Cambridge University Press, 1994), 165, 169 [161–175]. Further, O'Sullivan points out that Joye was less interested in creating a 'perfect' translation than getting any translation to the faithful as quickly as possible ("Bible Translations," 35). In contrast, Simpson notes Tyndale's insistence that the scriptural translation be sufficient, while at the same time producing voluminous reading aids that insist they too are necessary; we might note how Joye's translation style fulfills this goal in practice: James Simpson, "Sixteenth-Century Fundamentalism and the Specter of Ambiguity, Or the Literal Sense is Always a Fiction," in *Writing Fundamentalism,* eds. Axel Stähler and Klaus Stierstorfer (Cambridge, UK: Cambridge Scholars, 2009), 144 [133–154].

[46] George Joye, *An apologye made by George Ioye to satisfye (if it maye be) w. Tindale* ([Antwerp, widow of C. Ruremond], 1535), STC 14820, fol. C7r, "I wolde the scripture were so puerly & plyanly translated that it neded nether note/ glose nor scholia/ so that the reder might once swimme without a corke." Vivienne Westbrook makes much of Joye's opposition to apparatus in comparison to Tyndale: *Long Travail and Great Paynes: A Politics of Reformation Revision* (Dordrecht: Kluwer Academic Publishers, 2001), 2–3.

text clearer to circumvent the need for marginal helps."[47] This theory of translational pluralism situates Joye at once firmly within a medieval tradition, and squarely at the forefront of the evangelical valorization of *sola scriptura*. Further, it places him at odds with Tyndale.

FLAME WAR,[48] OR WHEN HACKERS FIGHT

From late 1534 into 1535, Tyndale quarreled with Joye over intellectual ownership customs, an argument with reverberations that may be felt in martyrologist John Foxe's denigration of Joye, a dismissal that plays a role in modern devaluation of him.[49] As we have already seen, initially Tyndale requested the assistance of the entire community of translators to aid in revising his text, but by 1526 he had revised his statement considerably to insist firmly that he alone would produce the revision. The trouble was that no revision was forthcoming for nearly a decade, and the pressure to reprint this smash hit was enormous.

The Worms edition printed by Peter Schoeffer sold out almost immediately, and was thereafter reprinted by another press, that owned by Christoffel van Ruremund (or van En-

---

[47] Westbrook, *Long Travail*, 3.

[48] The *New Hacker's Dictionary* gives the following definition for "flamewar"—"an acrimonious dispute, especially when conducted on a public electronic forum": Eric S. Raymond, *The New Hacker Dictionary* (Cambridge, MA: The MIT Press, 1996), 193. See also his definition of the verb form "to flame" as "to post an email message intended to insult and provoke," and "[such a post] directed at a particular person or people." It is worth noting that under the definition of "to flame," Raymond cites Chaucer (*Dictionary*, 193).

[49] Tyndale also quarreled with his sometime-aid William Roye, though that spat had fewer repercussions. See Guido Latré, "*The Newe Testament As It Was Written and Caused to Be Written, by Them Which Herde Yt* [tr. William Tyndale], ([Worms, Peter Schoeffer], [1526])," in *Tyndale's Testament*, eds. Paul Arblaster, Gergely Juhász, and Guido Latré (Turnhout: Brepols, 2002), 148–149. For Foxe's corresponding glorification of Tyndale, see King, "Light," especially 76–78.

dhoven) in Antwerp.[50] Already notorious for printing Dutch Lutheran bibles in 1526, the van Ruremund press was a natural alternate press for English scripture printing; the van Ruremunds had the presses, the pressmen, and the experience in printing such large (and risky) jobs.[51] For all their heavy investment in printing Catholic service books for English use, the van Ruremunds also appear to have had a religious interest in reform.[52] The van Ruremund press set to work immediately and produced a run of the 1526 edition by November.[53] Then years passed but no revision came. The van

---

[50] A complete account of the van Ruremund press remains to be written. For short overviews, see A.A. Den Hollander, *De Nederlandse Bijbel Vertalingen 1522-1545* (Niewkoop: De Graaf Publishers, 1997), 68–71, and also Andrew G. Johnston and Jean-François Gilmont, "L'imprimerie et la Réforme à Anvers," in *La Réforme et le Livre*, eds. Andrew G. Johnston and Jean-François Gilmont (Paris: Cerf, 1990), 201 [191–216].

[51] One of the van Ruremund Dutch bibles remains on various indices of prohibited books until 1571, decades after Christoffel's death. For a comprehensive list of prohibitions, see Fr. Heinrich Reusch, *Die Indices Librorum Prohibitorum des Sechzehnten Jahrhunderts* (Tübingen: H. Laupp, 1886). Antwerp already had a ban on Lutheran books. Frederick C. Avis argues strongly for the size and quality of the van Ruremund establishment: "England's Use of Antwerp Printers, 1500-1540," *Gutenberg-Jahrbuch* (1973): 238 [234–240]. For an overview of printing in Antwerp, see Johnston and Gilmont, "L'imprimerie et la Réforme à Anvers," 191–216. For an overview of printing in the Low Countries generally, see Andrew G. Johnston, "L'imprimerie et la Réforme aux Pays-Bas 1520-c.1555," in the same volume, 155–185, where there is a brief overview of Antwerpan book-bans on 182.

[52] The van Ruremunds are frequently cited as heavily invested in the English export market, and the prominence of their English New Testaments was noted by authorities more than once. For just a few examples, see the articles cited above in note 51.

[53] See Juhász's defense of this timeline in *Translating*, 276–277, and "Neglected," 3–4. The 1526 date can be corroborated thanks to Cardinal Wolsey's mass collection and burning of all English New Testaments found over the summer; van Ruremund's fall printing raised Wolsey's awareness of the printer as a source of English tes-

Ruremunds reprinted the 1526 edition again between 1530 and 1531; traveling to London to sell these copies led to Christoffel's imprisonment where he died in 1531. Printing bibles like this posed several serious risks. First and foremost, the English Bible was illegal, and those printing and selling it risked execution.[54] In addition, the printing cost had to be met up front, and recouped only later.[55] Meanwhile a large printing job like a New Testament could tie up a shop's presses and pressmen for some time, requiring a printer put off or refuse smaller, cheaper, and less risky ventures. Yet the New Testaments sold out swiftly every time, and were clearly a tantalizing prize for the competitive Antwerp printers. Christoffel van Ruremund's widow, Catherine, continued the business after her husband's death, and by 1533 she was ready to print another edition of the New Testament.

The story so far can be corroborated by outside sources; from here we can only rely on Joye's own account of events, and must use a pragmatic understanding of the early print industry to assess his claims. By 1533 two editions had been

---

taments.

[54] See Reusch in note 51 above for a list of prohibitions. For the 1527 prohibition of English New Testaments in Antwerp, likely suggested by the appearance of van Ruremund books, see Andrew Hope, "Ban on Possession of English New Testaments, Antwerp 1527," in *Tyndale's Testament,* eds. Paul Arblaster, Gergely Juhász, and Guido Latré (Turnhout: Brepols, 2002), 151–152.

[55] John Foxe recounts an amusing anecdote about a mercer tricking Bishop Cuthbert Tunstall into financing Tyndale's bibles: in an effort to suppress them, he used the mercer as a factor to buy all that the mercer could find in Antwerp. The books were burned, and a new printing of them occurred swiftly thereafter. As Foxe says, "the Byshop of London had the bookes, [the mercer] had the thankes, and Tyndall had the money": *Acts and Monuments* (London: 1570), 1159. See the scholarly edition of *John Foxe's Book of Martyrs* here: http://www.johnfoxe.org/ (accessed May 18, 2014). My thanks to Mark Rankin for recalling this episode to mind. Daniell says that Andrew Hope suggests that Christoffel van Ruremund received this payment (and offered up his books), rather than Tyndale, in *The Bible in English* (New Haven: Yale University Press, 2000), 145.

printed at the van Ruremund shop that employed no English-readers at all. In the early print world, even with expert copyeditors errors multiplied with every issue, and with no anglophone copyediting at all over multiple editions a canny printer like Catherine could have guessed that her copy might be corrupt enough to harm her profit-margin. Joye claims that she set about finding an Englishman familiar with the translation to correct her copytext.[56] A substantial printer, Catherine went straight to the top, according to Joye, and asked Tyndale himself to correct his own text: Tyndale refused. The English Nation in Antwerp was centered on the English House in Bullincstraat, and print shops were located in the nearby Cammerstraat and Lombaerdevest.[57] There is little doubt that had an offer been made, it would have been public knowledge among the expatriots and printers quickly. Catherine then asked Joye, who turned her down also.[58] She printed another error-ridden edition anyway. By 1534 that edition had sold out, and she prepared to print a fourth edition. She asked Tyndale to copyedit again, was turned down again, asked Joye again, and after some haggling he accepted.[59] The van Ruremund edition of 1534 was released with Joye's revisions, and Tyndale responded with barely bridled fury.

Tyndale hurried to complete his own thorough revision of the 1526 New Testament, and in the resulting 1534 New Testament added a second preface in which he accused Joye of a range of maleficence. Tyndale's anger at Joye concentrates on several allegations. The first is that "Joye revised

---

[56] Joye, *Apologye*, fols. C4r–v.
[57] Paul Arblaster estimates that at any one time in Antwerp, there were only about a hundred Englishmen resident. Numbers inflated significantly for the two annual fairs, at which he suggests 3–600 English might be present. For these statistics and information about the English House, see Paul Arblaster, "Domein de Waghemaker? Front Elevation of the English House," in *Tyndale's Testament,* eds. Arblaster, Juhász and Latré, 80–81.
[58] Joye, *Apologye*, fols. C4v–5r.
[59] Joye, *Apologye,* fols. C54–6r.

[the 1526 Testament] secretly . . . and persecuted me in printing large numbers of this correction before mine was released" despite the fact that "he knew that I was revising it myself."[60] He berates Joye for altering his text and not adding his name to it: "anyone who wishes may translate it and display his intellect, though a thousand had translated it before him. But it is not acceptable, I think, that someone takes another man's translation on his own authority and revises it wherever he likes and calls it a corrected edition."[61] The most damaging part of his argument lies in his charges that Joye persistently altered Tyndale's vocabulary regarding the resurrection of souls, a revision with serious theological ramifications.[62] In the end, Tyndale reiterates in striking language his theory of intellectual property, a theory that has been taken as justified by scholars for so long, despite being so unique at the time that it deserves to be quoted at length. Critics of his translation should respond thusly, according to Tyndale:

> And where they find faults, let them show them to me if they are nearby or write to me if they are far away, or write openly against it and improve it and I promise them if I agree with their reasons I will confess my ignorance openly. Therefore I beseech George Joye and all others too to translate scripture for themselves, either out of Greek, Latin or Hebrew. Or if they must, as the fox challenges the badger when he pisses in the badger's den, let them take my translations and labor at their pleasure and

---

[60] T1534, fol. **4r, "Joye secretly toke in hand to correct [the 1526 Testament] . . . and persecuted me/ in so moche/ that his correccyon was prynted in great nombre/ yer myne begane," "he knew that I was in correctynge it myselfe."

[61] T1534, fols. **4v–**5r, "it is lawfull for who will/ to translate and shew his mynde / though a thousand had translated before him. But it is not lawfull (thynketh me) . . . that whosoever will/ shall by his awne auctorite/ take another mannes translacion and put oute and in and chaunge at pleasure/ & call it a correccion."

[62] T1534, fol. **4v. Juhász has thoroughly disputed the veracity of these allegations ("Neglected," 8–40).

revise, edit, and corrupt it and call it their own translation and put their own names on it and not play Bo Peep as does George Joye.[63]

Such a biting indictment would cause many to pause, however learned in Greek, Latin, or Hebrew, before editing or translating scripture into English, much less writing to Tyndale personally with criticism. Whether the flame of martyrdom or the fire of Tyndale's displeasure, one risked much in daring to translate scripture into English.

Joye responded, first in a brief epilogue to Catherine van Ruremund's 1535 reprint of his corrected copy, and later that year in his full-length, printed *Apologye*. I believe that each response was carefully tailored to a different audience. The epilogue directed its comments to a broad audience including other hackers and general readers alike. In his initial rebuttal, like a hacker, Joye requests judgment of his peers: "I not only gladly consent [to be corrected] . . . but desire they all to judge, assess, and test all the scripture translation that I have ever or shall ever make."[64] Joye does not limit this group

---

[63] T1534, fols. **7r-v, "And where they fynde fautes/ let them shew it me/ if they be nye/ or wryte to me/ if they be farre of: or wryte openly agaynst it & improve it & I promyse them/ if I shall perceave that there reasons conclude I will confesse myne ignorance openly. Wherefore I beseche George Joye/ ye & all other to/ for to translate the scripture for themselves/ whether oute of Greke/ latyn or hebrue. Or (if they wyll nedes) as the foxe when he hath pyssed in the [badger's] hole chalengeth it for his awne/ so let them take my translacions & laboures/ & chaunge & after/ & correcte & corrupte at their pleasures/ and call it their awne translacions and put to their awne names/ and not to playe boo pepe after George Joyes maner." Tyndale later concludes that "I nether can ner will soffre of anye man/ that he shall goo take my translacion and correct it without name/ and make soche chaungynge as I myself durste not do" (fol. **7v) in utter disregard for the practicality of such a statement.

[64] *The hole new Testament with the Pistles taken out of the olde Testament to be red in the chirche,* ed. George Joye (Antwerp: Catharyn wydowe [of C. Ruremond], 1535), STC 2827 (hereafter to be abbreviated, J1535), fol. C7r, "I do not onely gladly consent there to/ . . .

like Tyndale does. Unlike Tyndale, he admits for community policing of standards. To the general audience Joye addresses words calming to ruffled consciences. He insists that readers make use of both Tyndale's and his own work, and further claims that this dispute "warn[s] us that we depend not solely on any one man's translation or his interpretation of doctrine, nor that we be sworn or addicted to any one man's learning, however holy and devout his speech."[65] This skepticism about the plenitude of any one translation is entirely absent from Tyndale's rhetoric, as is the direct engagement of the audience as a reading community of which the hacker is a part.

When Tyndale released his corrected edition in 1535, and simply removed the second, offensive preface without addressing himself to Joye's tarnished reputation, Joye responded by publishing a detailed, lengthy academic slander of Tyndale in his *Apologye*.[66] I argue that this reply was aimed directly at the evangelical community of translators, that is, at other hackers. In a real sense, this is an example of sixteenth-century flame war, or the arguments between hackers that occur in text-based, usually online formats. Juhász has noted the scholarly organization and approach of the *Apolo-*

but desyer them all to iuge/ expende and trye all that ever I have or shall wryte/ by the scriptures."

[65] J1535, fols. C7v–8r, "warne[s] us that we depende not wholl upon any mannis translacion nor hys doctryne nether to be sworne nor addicte to any mannis lerning/ make he never so holy and devoute protestacions."

[66] Raymond notes how important reputation among one's peers is to hackers, and Joye demonstrates this in several ways. He asks for (and presumably would accept) their judgment of his work and he structures his *Apologye* in an academic fashion, most accessible to his peer-hackers (*The Cathedral and Bazaar*, 241–242). For discussion of the *Apologye*'s scholarly organization, see Gergely Juhász, "George Joye, An *Apologye Made By George Joye, to Satisfy, If It May Be, W. Tindale*, 1535, edited by Edward Arber (The English Scholar's Library 13; Birmingham, 1882)," in *Tyndale's Testament*, eds. Arblaster, Juhász and Latré, 161, and Juhász, "Neglected," 15, 22–23, 30.

gye, and how it would have been difficult (and continues to be) for a reader not steeped in the intellectual traditions of Joye's time to work through it.[67] This specificity alone suggests Joye was speaking to a limited audience. Moreover, the personal nature of the *Apologye* suggests that Joye himself may have funded its printing, and given how impecunious the exile was, particularly after losing friends in the months of dispute with Tyndale, the print run for the *Apologye* could not have been large.[68] As a hacker, it is most likely that Joye wrote to other hackers to defend himself.

Joye's *Apologye* addresses hacker community customs that still resonate today. In it, he repeatedly contrasts his own preference for custom with Tyndale's unique promotion of a definition of intellectual property that imbricates authorship with editing and translation.[69] In contrast, Joye argues forcefully that he served as an editor only; he "corrected only the corrupted copy" for "the goodness of the deed and for the common profit."[70] Joye defines his concept of editing thusly: "as where I found a word incorrectly printed I fixed it, and when I came to some sentence so dark and difficult that no sense could be made of it, whether out of the ignorance of the first translator or of the printer, I had the Latin text by me and revised the sentence to be plain, and where any sentence was incorrect or entirely left out I restored it and gave many words their pure English meanings which they had not had before."[71] Joye signals his recognition of the limitations of

---

[67] Juhász, "Neglected," 30.

[68] Joye's loss of reputation and friends is noted by a contemporary; see Butterworth and Chester, *George Joye*, 194–197.

[69] Or as Simpson provocatively puts it, as it were ventriloquizing Joye, "Tyndale thinks he owns Scripture" (*Burning to Read*, 181).

[70] Joye, *Apologye*, fols. C3v, C5v, "correcked but the false copye," "the goodnes of the deede & comon profyte."

[71] Joye, *Apologye*, fol. C7r, "as where I founde a worde falsely printed/ I mended it: & when I came to some derke sentencis that no reason coude be gathered of them whether it was by the ignorance of the first transaltour or of the prynter/ I had the latyne text by me & made yt playn; & where any sentence was unperfite or clene left

editing when responding to Tyndale's attack on the anonymity of Joye's edition. Joye no more signed the edition than Tyndale himself did, Joye responds, and in any case, "should I have called it my translation for simply correcting the faulty and corrupt copy?"[72] The fact that Joye likely used the same Latin-Greek Bible that Tyndale employed argues further for his careful editorial method.[73] Joye wished to make clear to his audience of insiders that he was correcting corrupted code, not creating a "fork," that is, beginning an entirely new project on top of someone else's code, an action that we will see below is anathema in hacker circles.

Joye calls attention to Tyndale's disingenuous requests for revision, to how poorly he lived the customs of his community. "God forbid," Joye cries, "that Tyndale should think so much of himself to believe that he has perfectly, and on a first attempt, translated the New Testament, so that it cannot be improved, for he acknowledges and proves the contrary himself."[74] As we saw in Chapter 3, revision, development, was part of the long tradition of medieval biblical translation, a tradition in which Joye sees himself and Tyndale taking part. As Joye asserts, "I doubt not but that there is, and shall come after us, those who can and will correct our works and translations in many places and make them much more perfect and easier for a reader to understand."[75] In contrast, the de-

---

oute I restored it agene: & gave many wordis their pure & native significacion in their places which thei had not before."

[72] Joye, *Apologye*, fols. D4r–v, "shuld I have called yt my translacion for correcking the fawty & corrupt copye?"

[73] Jushász, *Translating,* 307.

[74] Joye, *Apologye*, fol. D5r, "God forbyd," "that T. shulde so think of hymselfe/ that he hathe so exquysitly/ (ye & that at first) translated the testament that yt cannot be mended/ for he aknowlegeth & proveth the contrary himself."

[75] Joye, *Apologye*, fols. D5v–5r, "I doute not but there be/ & shal come aftir us/ that canne & shall correcke our workes and translacions in many places & make them miche more perfayt & better for the reader to understande." Joye repeats this assertion again on fols. F6r–v.

gree of textual supremacy Tyndale claims for his translations was truly unique for a translator.

The dispute between Tyndale and Joye divides over the perceived breach of several significant customs relating to intellectual property that are similar to hacker practices today. First, we will see how the hackers today describe these customs. Then, we will see how Tyndale and Joye engage the same customs. Raymond notes that hacker communities share notions about property, and his outline of hacker property customs bears directly on the Tyndale-Joye spat:

- There is strong social pressure against forking projects. It does not happen except under plea of dire necessity, with much public self-justification, and with a renaming.
- Distributing changes to a project without the cooperation of the moderators is frowned upon, except in special cases . . .
- Removing a person's name from a project history, credits, or maintainer list is absolutely *not done* without the person's explicit consent.[76]

Tyndale felt that patches to his code, the revisions, should be his or by people he recognized, as he had asserted in his 1526 preface, and that Joye's were "rogue patches" of lesser quality and authenticity that might amount to a fork in the project.[77] Finally, Tyndale fumed that Joye had harmed his reputation, as Joye had not signed his work. Because the "success of a [developer]'s status is delicately dependent on the critical judgment of peers" to decouple a developer's name from his project is seen today as an aggressive, anti-communal act of appropriation.[78] Moreover, these acts of appropriation harm the entire community, not just the reputation of one developer.[79]

---

[76] Raymond, *The Cathedral and Bazaar*, 88 (emphasis in original).
[77] Raymond, *The Cathedral and Bazaar*, 89.
[78] Raymond, *The Cathedral and Bazaar*, 103–105.
[79] Raymond, *The Cathedral and Bazaar*, 105.

Yet in hacker communities "authority follows responsibility," and assessing whether or not Tyndale was taking responsibility for his project turns out to be a crux of the debate.[80] Joye claimed that Tyndale had turned down offers to copyedit this project for the van Ruremund press, and it is certain that he had failed to release a revised version in nearly ten years. From those facts it could be inferred that Tyndale was no longer taking responsibility for his text. To the rest of his community, it must have appeared that Tyndale was sanguine about his lack of control of the 1526 New Testament once it was first printed. The printing presses were not to be halted, as the van Ruremund editions attest. Financial or confessional, the pressure to print was incredibly strong. The commercial impetus behind the 1534 van Ruremund edition is crucial to recognize, so that scholarly rhetoric about Joye's "choice" to revise and print confuses two different operations.[81] It is doubtful whether George Joye could have stopped Catherine van Ruremund from printing another edition. The van Ruremund shop had sold thousands of copies of the 1526 edition already and there is not a single pragmatic reason to doubt another edition would roll off its press again whether or not Joye served as editor. Tyndale's quibble about timing, that the van Ruremund edition was printed in "large numbers . . . before mine was released" should be seen in its commercial light.[82] The printing houses knew what was on each others' presses and if Catherine knew she could put another several thousand New Testaments for sale before Marten de Keyser finished printing Tyndale's revision, so much the better for her.[83] Tyndale lashed out at Joye, but the printing was out of either of their hands, and the hackers among their audience knew it.

---

[80] Raymond, *Cathedral and Bazaar*, 125.
[81] Sadly, such rhetoric is altogether common; for a representative example, see Westbrook, *Travail,* 2, and the scholars using the term 'piracy' above on pages 85–86 of the present chapter.
[82] T1534, fol. **4r, "was prynted in great nombre/ yer myne begane."
[83] T1534, fol. **4r.

Given the way Catherine van Ruremund managed her shop, we have all the context we need to accept that the 1534 edition was going to be printed anyway, and support for Joye's insistence that he took the job to prevent truly confusingly corrupt copies, "bad code," if you will, from glutting the market and perhaps leading to confusion among readers. From Joye's perspective, and in Raymond's terms, Joye was attempting to *prevent* forking, not create it. Certainly the "project moderator," Tyndale, had not given his explicit permission to Joye's work, but he had apparently turned down the copyediting job himself, twice, and with a new edition in the works he had reasons for not taking on time-consuming, poorly-paid work. All of this opens up further ambiguity about how proprietary he felt about the old edition.

Among Raymond's list of hacker faux pas, that leaves us with removing a developer's name from the project. Uniquely, the opposite is true in this case; Tyndale insisted that by not accepting responsibility for the revision by signing his work Joye was playing "Bo Peep," and that without the new signature, readers would confuse the edition for Tyndale's own work.[84] Yet Tyndale did not sign his 1526 edition himself, and so Joye was following the existing code's architecture to the letter. This was architecture the hacker community knew well since it was traditional in the information commons, as we saw in Chapter 3.

Hacking Together a Complete Bible

The Bible continued to be hacked after 1535, but the era truly ended in 1549. English was officially promoted for use in religious matters. Tyndale was executed. The Pilgrimage of Grace polarized opinions across England. The Great Bible of 1539/40 was the first official, royally sanctioned translation, but the 1540s saw more evangelical books suppressed. How did this come to pass? Once Tyndale had been imprisoned

---

[84] T1534, fol. **7v.

and executed, hacker customs opened up several possibilities for the future of English bible development. To claim ownership of an existing project, one has to have that ownership transferred by a previous owner, or take over an abandoned project.[85] If "the only available measure of competitive success is reputation among one's peers," then Tyndale had by all measures succeeded, and those who took over development of his code, sadly abandoned, recognized that they stood on tall shoulders.[86]

Joye was not the only translator of his era to espouse traditional hacker values, values that were now under pressure from both institutional and cultural forces, as the twin threats of royal censure and Tyndale's anger demonstrate. Though they would not have met all of Tyndale's high criteria, there were many scripture translators and editors in the early sixteenth century, and like Joye, they all appear to have accepted the traditional information commons as a religious and commercial benefit. Editor William Marshall argues for the necessity of the scripture to be common, open, and free. Marshall expressed fear that the open, "light" and "truly translated" scripture is being kept closed, proprietary, out of the hands of the people, by the Church.[87] The printer Robert Redman's anonymous editor uses the rhetoric of common-

---

[85] Raymond, *The Cathedral and Bazaar*, 90–92.
[86] Raymond, *The Cathedral and Bazaar*, 99, 103.
[87] *A prymer in Englyshe* (London: Johan Byddell for Wyllyam Marshall, [1534]), STC 15986, fol. R5v, "the kynges hert is in thyne handes (Oh lorde) that where thou wylte thou mayest inclyne it . . . Inclyne his herte to this purpose (oh father) that it wyl please hym to commaunde his prelates of his realme no lenger to kepe from his people: his lovynge subiectes the lyght of thy worde, the lyght of holy scryptur . . . put it in his mynde lorde to commaunde that lyke as thrugh they secrete inspyration other nations already have: so his people also by his commaundement maye have in to theyr tonge truely translated thy holy scrypture." See Charles Butterworth, *The English Primers (1529-1545): Their Publication and Connection with the English Bible and the Reformation in England* (New York: Octagon Books, 1971), 65–66.

ness, freedom, and openness too.[88] For this editor the free circulation of these translations is required in order for the goal (in this case, proselytization) to be achieved. For him, the opening of the traditional religious texts into English out of the "Latin (which heretofore no one understood)" is necessary. Moreover, the text must be fully opened: to translate, to open, anything short of what was once closed is done not "so well as might have been." Sounding more like Joye than Tyndale, this editor also asks for the courtesy of emendation of his mistakes, "if any similar faults in this work have escaped either by negligence or out of ignorance . . . I humbly beseech you . . . to revise them charitably."[89] In the end, as Butterworth says, editors "felt perfectly free to range over the field before them and choose their readings from any source available to them."[90] We saw this traditional use of the information commons in Chapters 2 and 3. In contrast to Tyndale, Joye, Marshall, and Redman's editor all express and prove in actions that they understood scripture to be part of an information commons to which all English people had rights. Moreover, all of these men made use of Tyndale's text.

These three were lesser lights, however, and Coverdale

---

[88] *This prymer of Salysbery vse, bothe ein Englyshe & in Latyn* ([London]: Robert Redman, 1535), STC 15986.3, fols. +1v–+2r, "And for the more increase of vertue and avauncement of true doctryne they have now permyttyd and admytted suche prayours and suffrages as were wonte to be sayde and pronouncyd only in laten (which heretofore non dyd understande but only those that had the knowledge of the same tongue) to be translatyd into englysche. And of theyr blessyd zeale unto the increase of vertue and devocyon amonge people, where as heretofore none of the Prymars yet emprynted in englyshe hathe ben accordynge in al thinges unto the comon usage (to the entent that no man shuld be ignoraunt what he hathe said before time in laten). . . . In the settinge forth wherof, albehit that nether the translator nether the Pryntour have done theyre parte so wel as myghte have ben."

[89] STC 15986.3, fol. +4r, "if there be any like faultes in this work escapyd ether by neglygene or by ignoraunce. . . . I humbly beseche you . . . charitably to reform them."

[90] Butterworth, *Primers,* 98.

and John Rogers stepped in quickly as accepted successors to Tyndale's work at the very moment that the authorities began to support bible translation. Like the rest, Coverdale and Rogers, too, accepted an information commons. The Coverdale Bible was printed in Antwerp in October 1535, and the Matthew Bible (by Rogers) followed in 1537 in London with the initials "W.T." slipped into the text in surreptitious recognition of the developer on whose work Rogers built.[91] Above all Coverdale's source text is Tyndale: he included all of Tyndale's Old and New Testament translations, and filled in gaps with his own translation.[92] Rogers based his work on Tyndale's too, and he drew as well on Coverdale's translation.[93] Rogers' Matthew Bible is significant in being the first English bible to be licensed by the government. Following the printing of the Matthew Bible, English bibles might be considered legal. Further, the Matthew Bible in turn became the base text for the official Great Bible on which Coverdale served as editor. There was no textual ownership in evidence in either of these editions, but a community of developers honoring each others' work (such as by adding the "W.T." initials) and striving to improve it to fit new social and cultural conditions.

---

[91] The place of the Coverdale Bible's printing was confirmed by Latré, "Coverdale Bible," 89–102. For the "W.T." initials, see Daniell, *Bible*, 195.

[92] In his Bible, Coverdale shows awareness of Joye's translations, but bases his text on none of them. See Butterworth and Chester, *George Joye,* 58, 72, 122, 132, 138. This relationship is complicated by the fact that both used Zwinglian texts: Joye used Zwingli's Latin, and Coverdale used the Swiss-German Zurich Bible of 1534 (Butterworth and Chester, *George Joye,* 123, 125). See Guido Latré, "*Biblia. The bible,* translated by William Tyndale and Miles Coverdale, edited by Miles Coverdale (n.p., [Antwerp, Merten de Keyser?], 1535)," in *Tyndale's Testament,* eds. Arblaster, Juhász and Latré, 143–145, and Hobbs, "Martin Bucer," 151.

[93] For Daniell's convincing argument that Rogers recovered previously unpublished translation among Tyndale's papers, see *Bible,* 190.

In light of the recent argument between Tyndale and Joye, it is notable how very much Coverdale aligns himself with the traditional information commons in his 1535 prologue. "Though some men think that the existence of many translations makes division in the faith and among the people of God, this is not so," Coverdale insists.[94] Competition, Coverdale continues, makes for better translations.[95] As if in direct response to Tyndale's second preface against Joye, Coverdale pleads for understanding: "I took it upon myself to publish this special translation, not as an assessor, nor as a reprover, nor as a despiser of other men's translations, but I have followed previous interpreters humbly and faithfully, and did so subject to revision."[96] This is in balance part of what Joye argues in his *Apologye*. Further, Joye's statements about the importance of multiple translations ring through in Coverdale's belief that "there comes more knowledge and understanding of scripture through their diverse translations. . . . For where one interprets something obscurely in one place, the same person translates it elsewhere more clearly using a more plain term meaning the same thing."[97] Neither Coverdale nor Joye claim any ownership over their words: they are confident that others will come after and develop their code further. For Coverdale and Joye, "with enough

---

[94] Miles Coverdale, *Biblia the Byble, that is, the holy Scrypture of the Olde and New Testament, faithfully translated in to Englyshe* (Antwerp, 1535), STC 2063.3, fol. +4v, "Where as some men thynke now that many translacyons make divisyon in the fayth and in the people of God, that is not so."

[95] STC 2063.3, fol. +5r.

[96] STC 2063.3, fol. +5r, "I toke . . . upon me to set forth this speciall translacyon, not as a checker, not as a reprover, or despyser of other mens translacyons . . . but lowly & faythfully have I folowed myne interpreters, & that under correccyon."

[97] STC 2063.3, fol. +6v, "there commeth more knowledge and understonginge of the scripture by theyr sondrie translacyons. . . . For that one interpreteth somthynge obscurely in one place, the same translateth another . . . more maifestly by a more playne vocable of the same meanyng in another place."

eyes, all bugs are shallow."[98] That is, an information commons allows for the easiest development of quality translation.

While not entirely foreclosing bible hacking in the future, with the printing of the Great Bible the period of treating the text of the Bible as common, open, and free came to an end. Now there was an established text, authorized by the government. The Great Bible was open and would become common, but it was hardly free in the way the spate of printed scripture had been since 1526. The government's intention to control scriptural text was quickly clear. The Six Articles of 1539 had already signaled the rising power of a conservative response and in 1543 the backlash against the English Bible found parliament passing the "Act for the Advancement of True Religion" that severely restricted bible reading to the upper classes.[99] There would not be another edition of the Great Bible until 1549.[100] Apparently victorious, in some ways the hackers had lost. English people had the scripture, the law of God, in the common tongue, and this law was to be available in all parish churches. Yet one version alone was authorized. In the future, other translations would be made but the freedom of the traditional information commons was no more. One could borrow the scriptural text, but after 1540, generally it would be from one, official translation.

The squabble between Tyndale and Joye provides a case study of the range of pressures coming to bear on the information commons in the 1530s and 1540s. In combination, these pressures were powerful enough to lay down a cultural layer over the information commons, and restrict it to a degree never before seen. This activity was profoundly cultural, however. Without the cooperation of government and hackers, and perhaps the new practices associated with humanism, such an occurrence would never have taken place. While

---

[98] Raymond calls this "Linus's Law" (*The Cathedral and Bazaar,* 41).
[99] SoR, III:894–897.
[100] STC 2079.

these events did not result in modern copyright, or even a modern notion of intellectual property, the foundations for such development were now beginning to be laid, and a new cultural stratum was developing.

The hurdles to a printed translation of the law of man, of the statutes, were considerably different than those to an English bible, and it is to these that we will turn in Chapter 5. In the end, a similar cooperation of forces succeeded in closing down this portion of the information commons at about the same time as translating the Bible was successfully restricted. Rogers unwittingly points the way in the letter to Henry VIII preceding the Matthew Bible where he uses the importance of knowing the law of the land to argue for the necessity of the English Bible: "what wholesome and Godly laws such a king would endeavor to establish by which the law of God might better be observed . . . a Prince could not but will his subjects to read and follow all points of that law which he himself was so straitly bound both to keep and to read.[101]

---

[101] John Rogers, *The Byble which Is all the holy Scripture: in whych are contayned the Olde and Newe Testament truly and purely translated into Englysh by Thomas Matthew* (London: Grafton and Whitchurch, 1537), STC 2066, fol. *5v, "what wholsome and Godly lawes soche a kynge wolde indevoure hymselfe to enstablyshe/ by which the lawe of God myght the better be observed . . . a Prynce coulde not but will his subiectes to reade & folowe all the poyntes of that lawe/ which he him selfe was so strayghtly bounde both to kepe & reade."

CHAPTER 5: SELLING THE STATUTES

❧

The stakes were different in legal translation than they were in scripture translation because legal translation could not lead a hacker to martyrdom. Today it would be laughable to call an edition of a collection of laws a bestseller. Yet in the 1520s and 1530s several were. No less than the Wycliffite Bible discussed in Chapter 3 or the Reformation bibles explored in Chapter 4, in this chapter we will study translations made outside of institutional offices that became popular. More like the Great Bible than the Wycliffite Bible, however, these translated statutes eventually came under proprietary control of patents, and we cease to see the innovation of the previous century again after the 1540s. In the law as in scripture, the information commons came to be gated, and while many could benefit from its products, only the privileged few could manipulate its texts. Until that point, however, printers and translators we can only describe as activist, as "hacktivist" if you will, labored to open the entirety of statute law into English and to print these collections so that they might circulate freely. The common people bought thousands of them.

Unlike the English Bible, where royal interest trailed that of the hackers, the king pursued the Englishing of the law no less avidly than the hackers. In 1490 Henry VII had the statutes from his first several parliaments printed in English, and he was the first king to do so.[1] In 1504, Henry created the office of King's Printer, with the goal of having a printer always ready to produce official materials, and the position achieved real community recognition in 1508, when the Norman immigrant Richard Pynson took on the job. Nevertheless, while being the King's Printer gave Pynson ostensible privileges in legal printing, other printers sought ways around this restriction (more customary than legislated) from the beginning.[2] Below we will consider watershed translations that circumvented privileges of the King's Printer. As the 1520s wore on more concerted efforts at statute translation began to coalesce slowly, led by reformed law printers. In 1519, the lawyer and printer John Rastell translated and printed an alphabetical abridgment of all of the statutes up to Henry VII. The *Great Abridgement* went through five editions before Rastell's death in 1536, and three editions after. It qualifies as an early Tudor bestseller. From 1530 to 1534 Robert Redman used a fifteenth-century English translation to print the statutes dating from Edward III to Henry VII in English. He also hired the young George Ferrers, future courtier and author, to translate the statutes predating Edward III. With these three texts providing all of the medieval statutes in English, both in full-text and abridged and organized by topic, the statutes were opened to the common people, and they could circulate freely in an unprecedented way.

Of interest is the evangelical, hacker rhetoric used in the prefaces to these sixteenth-century translations, rhetoric em-

---

[1] For the reasons behind this, see Kathleen E. Kennedy, "Prosopography of the Book and the Politics of Legal Language in Late Medieval England," *Journal of British Studies* 53 (2014): 565–587.

[2] Baker reminds us that the king's printer received "a modest stipend" but "conferred no privilege in relation to law books generally."

phasizing the commonness of the statutes and the necessity that they be opened into English so that they could more freely circulate among the citizens. This rhetoric is identical to that which we saw in the Wycliffite Bible's General Prologue and in various religious texts in Chapter 4. It is not clear from where this re-emergence of hacker rhetoric in legal texts derives. Both religious and legal translations include hacker rhetoric beginning in the late 1510s, so we cannot point to the Reformation as a sole source, as the rhetoric appears early, and in (at the time) unreformed circles first. This provides yet another example of how the information commons formed an integral part of late medieval English culture. As we saw in Chapter 4, only a combination of forces was powerful enough to successfully alter it.

By the 1540s, the medieval tradition of an information commons was coming to an end, as we saw in Chapter 4. The cultural layer silencing the commons described there applies also to legal translation, and occurred in a similar fashion, if not with the same intensity. The Great Bible signified successful governmental control over bible translation and printing. However, in the 1550s the information commons was firmly closed by a group of printers who specialized in legal texts. Just as Bible translation was gated with the cooperation of Coverdale and Rogers, it was legal printers themselves who worked to restrict the commons. With the development of the Law Patent and the incorporation of the Stationers' Company, book production came under internal trade control exercised with royal support. For the first time in history, a layer of control could be exercised over the information commons.

Legal Evangelical John Rastell

More enterprising than most, John Rastell's innovations in information technology set new standards in legal literature and his rhetoric when discussing these innovations was decidedly activist in tone. Despite being most known for his dramatic works and as a translator, editor, and publisher,

Rastell is also responsible also for some of the most significant works of legal printing of the first half of the sixteenth century, and through them of the sixteenth century as a whole.[3] The brother-in-law of Thomas More, he was a lawyer of the Middle Temple and dabbled seriously in both printing and drama. Peter Herman describes Rastell thusly:

> although he is primarily known today as the author of dramatic interludes as well as two prose works, *The Pastyme of People* (1529) and *A new boke of Purgatory* (1530), he also participated in religious controversies, served as a government lawyer, helped design the Field of the Cloth of Gold and other political spectacles, tried to be the first Englishman to colonize the New World, and designed the first permanent theater in England.[4]

Following his conversion to the evangelical faith about 1532, Rastell's fortunes declined, and he died penniless in prison after nearly a year of incarceration in 1536. While he was not equally successful in his many endeavors, Rastell was a "Renaissance man" and innovation for the common profit was the heart of his enterprise.

Rastell did nothing by halves, and he was emphatic about access. For him the law was common and should be open and free, and he took it upon himself to move this process along. Rastell's interest in abridgment suggests an intense desire on his part to facilitate access to common information, a desire

---

[3] Peter Herman, "John Rastell (*London: 1509?-1536?*) William Rastell (*London: 1539-1534*)," in *The British Literary Book Trade, 1475-1700,* eds. James Bracken and Joel Silver (Washington, DC: Gale, 1996), 213. For more biography of Rastell, see E.J. Devereux, *A Bibliography of John Rastell* (Montreal: McGill-Queen's University Press, 1999), 17, 21–22. For an extended argument for Rastell's significance among legal theorists through the Civil War, see Richard Ross, "The Commoning of the Common Law: The Renaissance Debate Over Printing English Law," *University of Pennsylvania Law Review* 146 (1998): 323–461.

[4] Herman, "Rastell," 213.

that I think may have been developed in his years at the Middle Temple (sometime in the 1490s) watching Henry VII and later Edmund Dudley at work enforcing royal prerogatives and statutes as a means of improving regime finance.[5] Rastell was an utter barrister by 1502, just in time to see Henry's financial exploitation of the statutes at its most aggressive, and it was an experience that appears to have been formative.[6] Moreover, thanks to his family in Coventry, Rastell had ties with many of Henry's council learned, the heart of Henry's financial enterprise. Henry VII recommended Richard Empson, Edmund Dudley's chief accomplice, for the Coventry recordership in 1490, and he remained recorder until his imprisonment in 1509.[7] This position would have found Empson traveling between Coventry and the capital frequently, and he would have been well placed to notice Rastell, either at his old school the Middle Temple, or when Rastell (following in his father's footsteps) served as Coventry's coroner in 1507 and 1508.[8] Anthony Fitzherbert, eventually Chief Justice, took over as Coventry's recorder from 1509-1512, by which time Rastell was in the service of Edward Belknap.[9] Belknap was another member of Henry VII's council learned who had worked with Dudley and Empson direct-

---

[5] I think this far more likely a motivator than the *Supplication of the Commons* suggested in Howard Jay Graham, "'Our Tong Maternall Maruellously Amendyd and Augmentyd': The First Englishing and Printing of the Medieval Statutes at Large, 1530-1533," *UCLA Law Review* 59 (1965-1966): 70–71 [59–98].

[6] Cecil H. Clough, "Rastell, John," *Oxford Dictionary of National Biography* [ODNB], online.

[7] James Lee, "Urban Recorders and the Crown in Late Medieval England," in *The Fifteenth Century, Vol. 3: Authority and Subversion*, ed. Linda Clark (Woodbridge, UK: Boydell and Brewer, 2003), 171 [163–178]. See also references to Empson (or 'Emson') in *The Coventry Leet Book*, ed. Mary Dormer Harris (Early English Text Society: London, 1907-1913).

[8] See references to Rastell as coroner for these years in Harris, *Coventry Leet,* 604, 605, 619, 624.

[9] For Fitzherbert's service, see Harris, *Coventry Leet,* 628, 631, 635.

ly.[10] Rastell's position on the fringes of these powerful lawyers and officials who had been so intimately part of Henry VII's forceful use of statute law, a number of whom continued to be part of Henry VIII's administration, puts his work translating the statutes and making them more accessible for those outside the legal profession into stark perspective. Rastell was in a position to see the law used and abused at the highest levels, and had the activist streak that made him do something to (try to) improve the situation. As Devereux put it gently: "Rastell must have hoped that the press would point the way for the beginning of a better world . . . through reforms in law and legal education, the service of the commonwealth, and the printing and dissemination of good English books to serve good causes."[11]

Rastell's interest in increasing access to English law in order to protect the average person against rapacious exactions in the future is illustrated best by his *Great Abridgement,* an English abridgment of the statutes up to the beginning of Henry VII's reign organized topically in alphabetical order.[12] Clearly this was a tool for the common people. While many historians caution that Henry VII did not truly abuse the statutes at the expense of English citizens, the popular outcry against Dudley and Empson, the strong opinions of

---

[10] For Belknap's position on the council, see Mark Horowitz, "Policy and Prosecution in the Reign of Henry VII," *Historical Research* 82 (2009): 428 [412–458]. For Belknap as supervisor of the king's prerogative, see D.M. Brodie, "Edmund Dudley: Minister of Henry VII," *Transactions of the Royal Historical Society* 15 (1932): 158 [133–161]. For Rastell in Belknap's service, see ODNB, "Rastell, John" and Devereux, *Bibliography,* 7.

[11] Devereux, *Bibliography,* 6.

[12] Following Ames, Graham claims that Rastell printed an abbreviation of the statutes also in 1519; however, the preface he cites from Ames matches that of STC 9515.5 in all but typography. If 9515.5 is not the first printing of this text, it was the second of a now lost edition (or possibly, issue); there was no earlier abbreviation: Howard Jay Graham, "The Rastells and the Printed English Law Book of the Renaissance," *Law Library Journal* 7 (1954): 9n24 [6–25].

early historians, and Rastell's stated reasons for his popular legal works suggest a reaction against Henry's perceived excesses.[13] In 1519 the medieval statutes remained untranslated. The current acts of parliament had been printed in English since 1490, but this left hundreds of years of untranslated backlog. Therefore the *Great Abridgement* went some way toward filling a significant gap for those without ability in law French and Latin. Rastell approached his task with creativity and great skill. His translated abridgment had to be affordable, and easy to use even for people who lacked much formal education. Rastell printed the *Great Abridgement* as a tidy octavo in 1519, and expanded it in 1527. It was printed again by John's son William (probably for Robert Redman) in 1531, by Redman in 1528, 1533, 1538, then by Thomas Petit and William Middleton together in 1542, and its final edition was produced in 1551.[14] To have justified that many

---

[13] For historians cautioning against reading Henry's policies as simply new or extortionate, see for example, G.R. Elton, *England under the Tudors*, 3rd edn. (London: Routledge, 1991), 52; Horowitz, "Policy and Prosecution," 457–458; Mark Horowitz, "'Agree with the king': Henry VII, Edmund Dudley, and the Strange Case of Thomas Sunnyff," *Historical Research* 79 (2006): 364 [325–366]; and Margaret McGlynn, "'Of Good Name and Fame in the Countrey': Standards of Conduct in Henry VII's Chamber Officials," *Historical Research* 82 (2009): 547–549 [547–559].

[14] STC 9515.5, 9518 (John Rastell); STC 9521 (William Rastell); STC 9519, 9521a.5, 9522 (Redman); STC 9523 (Petit and Middleton); and STC 9525–9526 (Sears, Gaultier, and Powell). Cowley notes that STC 9521 is in types only used by William Rastell; however, as Redman printed the *Abridgement* both before and after William, and as we know that William printed another law book for Redman in 1531, I think it safe to claim that he was printing for Redman here as well: John D. Cowley, *A Bibliography of Abridgments, Digests, Dictionaries, and Indexes of English Law to the Year 1800* (Quaritch: London, 1932), xxiv–xxv. Cowley considers STC 9519 to be a different text, but even he admits it is nearly identical to Rastell's, and given the evident cooperation of William Rastell in subsequent years, I think we can consider this, as the STC does, one of the same series of editions (Cowley, *Bibliography*, xxvi).

editions, Rastell's English statute abridgment must have sold very well.

The translation involved in the *Great Abridgement* was itself a leap forward, but the volume also included apparatus to assist readers in using the text. Rastell's product development was thorough. In the initial edition, Rastell included a table of contents including all of the headwords in alphabetical order. Alphabeticization was still unusual enough in English texts that he included instructions for how it worked. Each subsequent edition featured improvements in the layout and range of finding aids.[15] Each of these elements worked together to assist readers in quickly accessing their law. All of this apparatus had been standard in scholarly texts for some time, but Rastell was among the first to use these technologies in an English-language text. The popularity of the *Great Abridgement* resulted in a wider dissemination of such information technologies as alphabeticization and the subject index than even the Wycliffite Bible had managed a hundred years earlier.

In scholarly texts these finding aids were ancient, and by bringing them to English law translations and putting them into print Rastell facilitated access for the general public and rendered the law more open and free. Nevertheless, Rastell imported and adapted these apparati from manuscript culture: they were not new to print as print historians Elizabeth Eisenstein and Howard Graham claim. "All show how new tools available to printers helped to bring more order and method to a significant body of public law," Eisenstein writes.[16] Indeed Rastell's adoption and further development

---

[15] The next addition of significant new apparatus occurred with William Rastell's edition, including a more strictly alphabetized table, numbered paragraphs, lists of expired statutes and new statutes, and a list of the statutory powers of the king and other officials: *The grete abbregement of the statutys of Englond vntyll the. xxij. yere of kyng Henry the. viij* [London?]: William Rastell, [1531?], STC 9521, fols. A3r-v.

[16] Elizabeth Eisenstein, *The Printing Press as an Agent of Change: Communications and Cultural Transformations in Early-Modern*

of the best medieval apparati in print was significant, but its significance lay partly in its translation into English and partly in the numbers of copies possible in print, rather than in pure novelty.[17] Graham overemphasizes the uniqueness of these improvements too: "unlike many Tudor law prefaces claiming innovations and revisions, those of the Rastells were not merely sales talk, but marked important stages in, and made important contributions to, professional legal training. Historically and methodologically, they recorded genuine improvements in the form and content of the lawbook."[18] Such information technologies were part of the scholastic tradition, and were found variously in the Wycliffite Bible and medieval statute collections in law French and English translation alike.[19]

Rastell prefaced his abridgment with the *Prohemium*, a defense of the law in English as common, open, and free that continued to be printed with the abridgment itself in all of the Rastells' three editions through 1531 and links Rastell's and Joye's translation theories. Rastell considers that "according to reason, every legal system by which any people are bound ought and should be written in such a manner and so openly published and declared that the people might soon,

---

Europe, 2 vols. (Cambridge, UK: Cambridge University Press, 1979), 105.

[17] Eisenstein, *Printing Press,* 105.

[18] Graham, "Rastells," 21.

[19] Mary and Richard Rouse are seminal in the area of scholastic apparatus: see their book *Authentic Witnesses: Approaches to Medieval Texts and Manuscripts* (Notre Dame: University of Notre Dame Press, 1991). For the paratexts in statute collections, see their chapter "Reading the Law: Statute Books and the Private Transmission of Knowledge in Late Medieval England," in *Learning the Law: Teaching and the Transmission of Law in England, 1150-1900,* eds. Jonathan A. Bush and Alain Wijffels (Rio Grande, OH: Hambledon Press, 1999), 123–128. For the elaborate paratexts available with the Wycliffite Bible, see Matti Peikola, "'First is writen a clause of the bigynnynge therof': The Table of Lections in the Manuscripts of the Wycliffite Bible," *Boletin Millares Carlo* 24-25 (2005-2006): 343–378.

without great difficulty, understand the same laws."[20] Here the commonness of the law is stressed: all are bound to it, and so all should have ready access to it. Here, too, we see the same concentration on openness that we saw in Chapters 3 and 4 concerning scriptural translation, and also the importance of free circulation.

Rastell's approach to translation is historically situated and pragmatic. Like Joye's, Rastell's historically relativist understanding of language demands repeated translations, not eternal canonical ones. In the *Prohemium,* Rastell launches into a history of the languages of the English law, noting that French used to be a more sufficient language for the law than English, but eventually became less well known. As a lawyer, Rastell was familiar with the Statute of Pleading, and in the *Prohemium* he spins this statute as an effort toward opening the law; with the records kept in Latin, "every man might understand it generally."[21] Yet for Rastell, as language changes over time, the law needs to be made available in an accessible language. Rastell's "everyman" audience is not truly populist, but he does open the law to a wider audience than previously, one familiar with Latin, but not the closed language of law French. It is Henry VII, "the second Solomon," who Rastell lauds as recognizing that "our vulgar English tongue was marvelously amended and augmented" thanks to the efforts of translators over the years, and could now be the vehicle for the law.[22] Rastell emphasizes at several points that Henry VII's decision to shift the language of the statute law into English creates a scenario whereby "all his liege people

---

[20] STC 9515.5, fol. [A]1r, "in reason every law whereto any people shuld be boundyn ought & shulde be wryttyn in such manere and so opynly publysshed & declaryd that the people myght sone wythout gret dyfyculte have the knoulege of the same laws"; *The statutes prohemium Iohannis Rastell* [London]: John Rastell, [1519].

[21] STC 9515.5, fol. [A]1v, "every man generally & indyfferently myght have the knolege thereof."

[22] STC 9515.5, fol. [A]2r, "our vulgare englysh tong was marvelously amendyd & augmentyd."

might understand it."[23]

The biblical Solomon was not above grave errors, and the years of Rastell's legal training in the Middle Temple put him in a good position to see the king's council learned at its controversial work. It does not seem coincidental that in his first law translation effort, Rastell's concern was to educate people about laws that could hurt them, "and so through that knowledge to avoid the danger and penalties of the same statutes," as it had been these same penalties that Henry VII's counselors had been so zealous to collect.[24] Henry VIII scaled back, but did not neglect this source of income. Therefore, Rastell concentrated his first edition on abridging those laws carrying forfeitures and penalties. By his second, expanded edition, he had abridged the entirety of the statute law to Henry VII's reign.[25]

A closed, proprietary law could only hurt the common people, and Rastell says so explicitly in his preface to the first English legal dictionary, echoing a famous fourteenth-century medieval lawyer:

> it follows that the law in every realm should be so published, declared, and written in such a way that the people bound to the same law might soon and quickly understand it. Otherwise a law kept secretly and in the knowledge of only a few people, kept from the knowledge of the multitude might rather be called a trap and a net to bring the people to vexation and trouble.[26]

---

[23] STC 9515.5, fol. [A]2v, "al hys lege people myght have the knolege thereof."
[24] STC 9515.5, fol. [A]2v, "and so by reason of that knolege to avoyd the dangere and penaltes of the same statutys." See W.C. Richardson, *Tudor Chamber Administration 1485-1547* (Baton Rouge: Louisiana State University Press, 1952), 157–158.
[25] Compare Rastell's description in STC 9515.5, fol. [A]2v and STC 9521, fol. A2v. The *Prohemium* is nearly identical edition to edition, but with slight expansion between the first and second editions, Rastell ensures that it still accurately reflects the contents.
[26] STC 2070.1: John Rastell, *Exposicio[n]es t[er]mi[n]o[rum] legu[m]*

In this wording Rastell comes close to quoting the popular fourteenth-century poet and lawyer John Gower, who in his *Vox Clamantis* had made an extended metaphor of the "net of the law" and claimed in part that "the greedy lawyer envelopes his trembling neighbors with the law and traps them. He oppresses timid people who have no defense, and binds them with the net of law. The innocent mob falls into his webs, and the lawyer's ruinous nets provide a way out for the man of prestige."[27] Both lawyers see the monopoly of the legal profession over the law as dangerous to the commons. It could not be more plainly expressed: for Rastell, a closed, propriety law that did not circulate freely was antithetical to good government and to ethical legal practice, and put the common people in direct jeopardy.

Like Joye's New Testament epilogue, in the *Prohemium* Rastell recognizes that he is speaking to a mixed audience of fellow law hackers and general public. Rastell exhibits some of the same concerns about his audience and the limitations of his text that Tyndale and Joye did, but he handles them in a much different way, thanks to the nature of his project. Unlike the scripture translators, Rastell asks his readers only pardon for errors, requesting that his readers "consider my good will, as I intended [the translation] for the common weal."[28] However, like Joye, Rastell also stresses the common

---

anglo[rum], London: John Rastell, [1523], fol. A1r, "it folowyth that the law in every realme shuld be so publysshyd, declaryd and wrytton in such wyse that the peple so bound to the same myght sone and shortely come to the knowlege therof/ or ellys such a law so kept secretly in the knowlege of a few persones and from the knowlege of the great multytude may rather be callyd a trape and a net to brynge the peple to vexacioun and trobyll."

[27] For simplicity's sake I quote from Stockton's translation, *The Major Latin Works of John Gower*, trans. Eric Stockton (Seattle: University of Washington Press, 1962), 221–222. Though the *Vox Clamantis* was not printed in the sixteenth century, it had been popular in the fifteenth century, and it seems likely that Rastell knew the work from a manuscript source.

[28] STC 9515.5, fol. [A]3r, "consyder my good wyl which have in-

good behind his project. Rastell encourages readers to double-check the statutes that he cites in any case of doubt, and his citations make this possible in many cases. This request betrays his diverse audience, however, as only others literate in Latin and law French could do that fact checking in 1519. Finally, in a wonderfully modern caveat, Rastell cautions readers to hire a professional lawyer if they need legal advice.[29]

In a sense, with this final warning, Rastell voiced an Early Modern version of hackers' claims today that an information commons leads to better business, not worse.[30] In 1998, the internet browser Netscape opened its source code, becoming Mozilla (developer of Firefox), which is now one of the top three internet browsers: it stands alongside Microsoft's proprietary Internet Explorer, semi-proprietary Google Chrome, and well ahead of fully proprietary Apple Safari.[31] The Android mobile phone operating system is semi-open and at the time of this writing, it is the most popular mobile phone operating system in the world.[32] The *Great Abridgement* did not take the place of the legal profession, but it was instead an inspired gap-filler. Common folk and legal profession alike, everyone benefited from the *Great Abridgement*.

tended yt for a comyn welth."
[29] STC 9515.5, fol. [A]3r.
[30] See, for example, Chapter 6 on the opening of Netscape and its transformation into Mozilla (now Firefox) in Eric S. Raymond, *The Cathedral and the Bazaar: Musings on Linux and Open Source by an Accidental Revolutionary* (New York: O'Reilly, 1999).
[31] See *StatCounter: Global Stats*, gs.statcounter.com (accessed May 18, 2014).
[32] As of this writing, Android exists in two forms. One is "pure" Android, and is open. The more common variant includes a proprietary "skin" of code created by the handset-maker on top of the open Android code. See, again, *StatCounter: Global Stats* cited in note 31 above.

ROBERT REDMAN, PIRATE PRINTER

The King's Printer since 1508, Richard Pynson had reason to call Redman "Rudeman," and Redman's treatment of Pynson is the closest we come in this book to modern intellectual piracy. Redman's actions can only be interpreted as aggressive. Possibly emboldened by anti-immigrant sentiment, Redman began printing identical legal material in time with Pynson.[33] Perhaps this was annoying to Pynson, but it was hardly exceptional.[34] Yet the pattern continued.[35] Things seem to have come to a head when Redman began printing a popular legal handbook on Pynson's heels.[36] Finally Pynson took Redman to task in a Latin letter to the reader appended to the law French handbook.[37] In this letter Pynson insists on the quality of his products' correction, typography, and decoration, and contrasts its quality with (in part) "that which escaped from the hand of Robert Redman, but more truly 'Rudeman,' because among a thousand men a ruder could by no means easily be found."[38] In particular, Pynson denigrates Redman's sloppiness when printing the "holy laws of the English."[39] In this letter we have something that looks a lot

---

[33] On community prejudice and Pynson's immigrant status, see William Kuskin, "'Onely Imagined': Vernacular Community and the English Press," in *Caxton's Trace: Studies in the History of English Printing*, ed. William Kuskin (Notre Dame: University of Notre Dame Press, 2006), 199–240.

[34] STC 9779, STC 9780.

[35] When Pynson printed the law reports of 9 Edward IV, Redman did too: see 9 Edw IV in STC 9826 and 9827, 12 Edw IV the year following in STC 9839 and 9838.7, and 14 Henry VIII in STC 9945 and 9944.5, for just a few examples.

[36] STC 23880, 15726, 15727, 15729.

[37] Thomas Littleton, *Lyttylton tenures newly and moost truly correctyd [et] amendyd*, [London: Richard Pynson, 1525], STC 15726, fols. Y8r–v.

[38] STC 15726, fol. Y8r, "quam elapsus est e manibus Rob. Redman, sed verius Rudeman, quia inter mille homines rudiorem haud facile invenies."

[39] STC 15726, fol. Y8v, "sanctas leges Angliae."

like Luther's frustrations with the printing business, only in this case it was straightforward competition between printers.

We have seen with Tyndale and Joye's dispute how hurling epithets was part and parcel of early printing, but Pynson's insistence on the quality of his own work speaks to his frustration with Redman's campaign of identity theft. Redman did not copy Pynson's nonlegal list, but his piracy was not limited to the texts themselves. Redman's strategy was more devious than that. Like many craftsmen, printers identified themselves by marks, and in printing this meant a characteristic woodcut. Redman began to infringe on Pynson's marks. One of Pynson's marks was the royal arms, crowned. Redman began to use the Tudor rose, crowned.[40] Pynson printed at the sign of the George on one side of Temple Bar, and Redman moved into premises at the sign of the George on the other side of Temple Bar.[41] In an almost Kafkaesque ending, when Pynson died Redman took over the old printer's shop, marks, and types.[42] Notably the office of King's Printer did not descend to Redman, but it went instead to another French immigrant, Thomas Berthelet (upon whose privileges Redman also infringed).[43]

---

[40] For examples in the *Tenures*, see STC 15728 and 23880.5

[41] See his colophon in STC 9618 and STC 17728.

[42] See, for example, Redman's use of Pynson's crowned royal arms on an edition of the *Tenures* printed just after Pynson's death in 1530, STC 15730. The contrast with Rastell's printing of the *Tenures* is important: Rastell printed the *Tenures* in bilingual editions in 1523 and 1525, matching Pynson's editions, but Rastell significantly developed Pynson's text by including a translation, and he printed them under his own, unique mark (STC 23879.7, 23880.3).

[43] Graham, "Our Tong Maternell," 79. Nevertheless, Pynson's justified ire may also have been the expression of a bruised ego and flat sales: J.H. Baker finds evidence that Redman's editions were superior to Pynson's, despite his undeniably inflammatory business model (Baker, *Oxford History*, 496). The dates Baker gives for these superior editions and his crediting of an anonymous editor lead me to wonder whether these are more work by George Ferrers, who we will discuss further below.

Reformed though not particularly evangelical, Redman covered his move into evangelical printing with a solid legal (in multiple senses) catalog, including Rastell's *Great Abridgement*. In the law too he was a reformer, and it was Redman who printed the first complete translations of the statutes from Edward III's reign onward, in *The Great Boke of the Statutes* (1530-1533) and the statutes predating Edward III in *The Boke of the Magna Carta* in 1534. For the bulk of the former, I contend elsewhere that Redman printed a translation originally made in the 1440s.[44] To make the latter translation Redman hired a law student with a bright future as copyeditor and later courtier and author, George Ferrers. Of the two books, it was the *Boke of the Magna Carta* that proved more popular, being printed first in 1534, then twice more, while the *Great Boke* was reprinted only once.[45] The folio size of the *Great Boke* and octavo size of the *Boke of the Magna Carta* must have helped sales of the latter as well. While not the bestseller that Rastell's *Great Abridgment* was, these volumes remain landmarks. With *The Boke of the Magna Carta* and *The Great Boke* the English finally had free access to their law in their own language for the first time in 500 years.

Not long after his death, Redman's widow, Elizabeth Pickering, printed the second edition of the *Boke of Magna Carta*. This edition added a letter to the reader about the necessity of having the statutes in English and thereby added another stratum to this work.[46] As we saw with Rastell's *Pro-*

---

[44] This translation is extant today in London, British Library, MS Harley 4999: see Kennedy, "Prosopography of the Book."

[45] These reprints were by Redman's widow in 1541, and by Thomas Petit in 1542 (STC 9286, 9272, 9275, 9276). The *Great Boke* reprint is STC 9287–9288, in 1542 by Middleton. The property appeared to be sound enough that Berthelet printed an "official" version in 1543, however, which ended the afterlife of Redman's copy. See *The great boke of statutes* (London: Robert Redman, 1533?), STC 9286, and *The boke of Magna Carta* (London: Robert Redman), 1534, STC 9272.

[46] This letter is believed to be by Ferrers, but I think we cannot as-

hemium, this preface appears to have struck a chord, or at least been perceived as commercially useful, as Petit includes it in his 1542 edition as well. Even more than Rastell's *Prohemium*, the letter prefacing *The Boke of the Magna Carta* addresses a dual audience of hackers and general readership. In a rather homey voice fond of idiomatic phrases, the copyeditor's solution to a flawed text contrasts starkly with Tyndale's. The copyeditor admits the difficulty of the task of translating the statutes, and suggests that errors be corrected, rather than the entire project repeated, due to the difficulty of law French and Latin: "take pains to reform such faults gently, for such a thing may sooner be dispraised than amended. For if this ice was to be cut again, men should find it no easy piece of work to take in hand, especially when many of the terms in French and Latin are so long out of use due to their antiquity."[47] This is standard development practice in an information commons, and we heard similar requests from Joye and Coverdale in the previous chapter. Recommending the further development of an extant project contrasts sharply with Tyndale's demand that his critics translate the Bible over again from scratch. The letter expects that law students will find the *Boke of the Magna Carta* useful, and it assures

---

sume this: years had passed since Ferrers made the original translation and in 1541 he was poised to be taken into royal service. He served as an MP in 1542. It is doubtful that he would have been interested in such a tedious and unremunerative job as correcting his old assignment at such a time, and it seems more likely that Redman or Pickering hired another young law student to make the revisions. For the attribution to Ferrers, see Graham, "Our Tong Maternall," 68.

[47] *The great Charter called i[n] latyn Magna Carta with diuers olde statutes whose titles appere in the next leafe Newly correctyd. Cum priuilegio. ad imprimendum solum* (London: Elizabeth Pickering, 1541?), STC 9275, fol. +2r, "take paynen gentylly to refourme [faults for] such a thyng as may be soner dypraysed then amendyd. For yf thys yse were to be cutte agayne/ men shulde fynde it no easy pece of worke to take in hand, specyally when many of the termes aswell French as latyn be so ferre out of use by reason of theyr antyquyte."

them that by careful study of the laws "a good student will soon attain perfect understanding."[48] Yet, a larger, more general audience appears to have been envisioned as well. We find that it is the commonness of the law that drove the copyeditor's work: "and because the greater part of the law retains its force and binds both king and subjects up to the present day, I thought it necessary to set them forth in a manner in which people might best understand them," an understanding they can not have if they are not opened into English, a language that the general audience can read.[49] "This is why this book was translated into English; though it will not satisfy the learned, yet it will be a good help for the unlearned": like Rastell, this writer acknowledges the legal insufficiency of the English statutes, while at the same time advertising their necessity for general audiences.[50] The statutes were common and needed to be open and free.

The information commons' gate closed more slowly for law than it did for scripture, but close it did eventually. Robert Redman's widow may have been instrumental in pulling the gate shut. The Law Patent was created in 1553 for Richard Tottell, and it continued to be a coveted monopoly after him. This patent gave Tottell the exclusive right to print all texts of the common law. Barbara Kreps argues that Elizabeth Redman's then-husband, Ranulph Chomeley, assisted Tottell in acquiring the patent.[51] With this patent leaving only one

---

[48] STC 9275, fol. +2v, "a good student shal soone attayne to a perfyte iudgement."

[49] STC 9275, fol. +2v, "and bycause the moste part of [the laws] retayne theyr force, and bynde the kyng & subiectes unto this day, me thought it necessary to set them forth in such sorte as men myghte beste have knowledge of them."

[50] STC 9275, fol. +2v, "For this cause I saye was this boke translated into the Englyshe, whiche though percase it shal not satysfye the lerned, yet shall it be a good helpe for the unlerned."

[51] Barbara Kreps, "Elizabeth Pickering, the First Woman to Print Law Books in England and the Relations Within the Community of Tudor London's Printer and Lawyers," *Renaissance Quarterly* 56 (2003): 1072 [1053–1088]. "Randle Cholmeley" entered Lincoln's

printer legally capable of printing English common law, the medieval legal information commons was no more. In Chapter 4 we saw that by 1553 the free development of Bibles had already eroded. There remained yet another large step before the information commons was fully smothered by this new layer of control: the Stationers' Company.

We saw in both Chapter 4 and the present chapter how printers had gotten around patents and privileges handily for decades. It took another innovation to firmly close the information commons. A group of printers incorporated, legal printers as it so happened, and the resulting Stationers' Company greatly increased the surveillance of printing in England. This was institutional censorship from the inside. Though not incorporated until 1557, efforts were underway as early as 1550, and once again, Ranulph Cholmeley was at the forefront.[52] An earlier attempt at incorporation was made as far back as 1542, and Elizabeth's previous husband William Cholmeley (brother to Ranulph) may have been involved with that effort.[53] It was the Stationers' Company who would demand that every printed work be licensed and en-

---

Inn in 1535. J.H. Baker, in "Roger Cholmeley," *Oxford Dictionary of National Biography* (online), notes that "Randle Cholmeley" was Roger's cousin, and a Recorder of London who died in 1563. For Elizabeth Pickering, see Alexandra Gillespie, "Robert Redman," *Oxford Dictionary of National Biography* (online): this notes that her last husband, "Ranulph Cholmeley" was a Recorder of London who died in 1563. It seems certain they are the same person. William Cholmeley, Elizbeth's penultimate husband, was admitted to Lincoln's Inn in 1528: *Records of the Honourable Society of Lincoln's Inn*, Vol. 1, ed. William Baildon (London: Lincoln's Inn, 1896), 49.

[52] Kreps, "Elizabeth Pickering," 1074–1075.

[53] Peter Blayney, *The Stationers' Company before the Charter, 1403-1557* (London: Worshipful Company of Stationers and Newspaper Makers, 2003), 41–42. Thanks also to Martha Driver for providing me the text of her conference paper, "'By Me Elysabeth Pykeryng': Women and Printing in the Early Tudor Period," Annual Meeting of the Modern Language Association, Philadelphia, Pennsylvania, December 27-30, 2009.

tered into the Company's register.[54] It was not copyright, but control over English printing the Stationers most certainly enforced. Not every printer would be so corralled, as John Wolfe's gleeful late-sixteenth-century piracies vividly illustrate, but the fact that Wolfe's case remains a standard example is notable. "Piracy" could exist only when the information commons was no longer normative.[55]

With the dawn of the 1540s, the medieval information commons was coming to an end, and by 1560 it was no more. The combined force of internal cooperation among translators and printers and royal regulation and enforcement exerted enough pressure over time to develop a complete layer of cultural sediment over the once-thriving information commons. A royally sanctioned translation of the Bible was available, and its printing was regulated and protected by patent. At the same time a group of legal printers and publishers were testing their power and laying the groundwork for what would become the Law Patent and the Stationers' Company itself. As we have seen, from the fourteenth century, scripture and the statutes were foundational texts of English culture. We might today call them popular media. Production of them was at-will, and cultural inertia was so strong that early attempts at canalizing the information commons were unsuccessful. Yet by the sixteenth century political and commercial power structures had changed enough that control of the information commons became possible. Hackers continued to go about their business, of course, but as did Wolfe,

---

[54] For bibliography on the early Stationers' Company, see Cyprian Blagden, *The Stationers' Company: A History, 1403-1959* (Stanford: Stanford University Press, 1960), and Blayney, *Stationers' Company*, 41–42.

[55] For Wolfe's case, see Chapter 2 of Joseph Lowenstein, *The Author's Due: Printing and the Prehistory of Copyright* (Chicago: University of Chicago Press, 2002).

they were now operating on the fringes of legality, erupting through the layer of information property. The modern world coined the term "hackers"—the Middle Ages did not because nearly everyone was one.

HOMO HACKER? AN EPILOGUE

Hackers and cyberpirates are categories of today, of the twenty-first century, and what this book explores is a moment in history when such behavior was the norm. The translators, copyists, and printers we have studied in this volume were all participating in a textual culture that regarded texts as the common property of all. Open and accessible to a general audience, these texts circulated freely. The medieval hackers used texts in the information commons, changed them to suit local needs, and released them out into the commons again, to be used and modified further by the next hacker in need of them. The technologies they were adopting and adapting—languages, information technologies like apparatus, and finally the printing press itself—reflected and affected the medieval hackers' code. Most of these people were not aware of these actions: it was simply their culture to handle texts as part of an information commons. However, in the face of institutional efforts to control the information commons, some hackers spoke out, and appear self-aware of their culture. The rhetoric they use in describing and defending this culture is the same rhetoric that hackers use today. Medieval hackers emphasized the commonness, openness, and freedom required for foundational texts in their culture just as modern hackers do. Nevertheless, in the end, the medieval information commons was closed. The hackers lost.

The printing press was a tool of this change, but not an agent of it. If hackers had not already pre-existed to take advantage of the press, a revolution could not have occurred. In geologic terms, we might think of the printing press as one chemical element that had the potential to be acted on in a range of ways, to produce different reactions. I think the revolution was not one of print, but of information technology more broadly construed. The gating of the traditional information commons was a true revolution. Members of the book trades themselves brought the information commons under institutional control, both external and internal. Despite being a hacker, Coverdale worked as an editor on the Great Bible, a Bible that would only ever be published by permission, and one that would swiftly come to be protected by royal privileges and patents. At some point in the early 1540s a group of powerful law printers began to develop the idea of a trade guild with control over all printing. In the 1550s this project became the Stationers' Company. The Stationers worked in tandem with the government, and formed a network of control. Today, our own code's horizons have expanded radically once again thanks to information technologies and the digital revolution, but institutional control has canalized much of our uses of this technology.

It may not be coincidence that at this cultural moment the notion of medieval information technology and Wyclif emerge back into our culture with a certain poignancy. The web comic *Married to the Sea* takes nineteenth-century engravings in the public domain and adds amusing captions to them, demonstrating the information commons across time and form, but also illustrating how far back one must go today to find public domain images. The comic of a monk copying a text places our current information culture in stark perspective.¹ The monk believes that he is good at copying, and he is the fastest copyist in his monastery: "I'm like a machine. A *copying machine*." Here is a response to Eisenstein's argument about the printing press as an agent of change in a single image and line of text. The scribe's swiftness was only a good thing, something of which to be proud as this monk is, if there was already an audience for the products of that machine-like copying. The printing press made mass duplication of texts possible, but the audiences were primed for that new mass of texts by the products of hand copyists before movable type was a gleam in Gutenberg's eye. The modern irony lies in the fact that this monk risks nothing in all of his copying because he lives in a culture with an information commons. Our copy machines, analog and digital, bring with them risks for us today, and so we romanticize the monk's pride in his swift work. We do not know what the monk in the comic is copying so quickly, but the text in question in modern invocations of John Wyclif, the Bible, is of deep cultural importance.

That "John Wyclif's" language hacking could be a topic in a webcomic called *Dinosaur Comics* in 2009 is a further example of recent interest in medieval information technology (Fig. 4).² The comic begins by calling audience attention to language change over time: "in the 1300s regular chicks and dudes in England were speaking what we'd call 'Middle English,' a rapidly developing alternative to the Latin and French used in government."

The comic addresses medieval concerns about English sufficiency that we have examined in this book: "and some of these dudes were big into English being developed as a 'real' language." In the comic, linguistic hurdles are directly related to institutional and political struggles:

---

¹ *Married to the Sea: A Sharing Machine Comic*, http://www.marriedtothesea.com. See also http://www.marriedtothesea.com/030707/copying-machine.gif.
² Ryan North, *Dinosaur Comics*, September 9, 2009, http://www.qwantz.com/index.php?comic=1548 (accessed 18 May 2014).

T Rex: But when they started translating, they ran into some problems!
Utahraptor: Papal resistance?
T Rex: That, but also a lot of English words they needed didn't exist yet!

Figure 4. reproduced with permission of Ryan North, *Dinosaur Comics*

The humor of the comic centers squarely on the twenty-first century wonder at a world without an English word for 'intestine' and the implied institutional resistance to creating an English word for 'intestine,' a world where linguistic poverty seems as serious as political resistance. This wonder crashes into embarrassment with the revelation that Wyclif's creative solution was 'arseropes.' Many of the computer-culture terms used in this present book are neologisms and it remains to be seen whether twenty-first century 'arseropes' or 'intestines' will triumph.

Mistakes in historical fact are made in these renewings of who Wyclif was and what he did, but the cultural work accomplished by this myth remains relatively unaffected by these errors. In actuality, while the *Middle English Dictionary* does credit the Wycliffite Bible as the earliest use of "arse-ropes," both the MED and the *Oxford English Dictionary* also attest the word "intestine" used from the same date.[3] As we saw in Chapter 3, Wyclif himself did not translate the Bible: yet both *Dinosaur Comics* and (at the time of this writing) Wikipedia continue to emphasize that he did.[4] "Medievalism" gets associated most frequently with the *romance* genre, but in *Dinosaur Comics* as in *Married to the Sea* we have medieval information technology being mythologized in a way that puts a single face on an information culture that is gone but not forgotten.

It seems that the twenty-first century wants a single hero to have translated the Bible, to have overcome both institutional and linguistic resistance. Far less self-conscious than *Dinosaur Comics* is the animatronic John Wyclif at The Holy Land Experience, a themepark in Orlando, Florida.[5] At Holy Land, as in *Dinosaur Comics*, Wyclif is identified as a translator of the evangelical Bible, and the modern mechanical and the medieval meet in the Holy Land's "Scriptorium: Center for Biblical Antiquities." This houses the Van Kampen collection, which includes parts of several Wycliffite New Testaments and part of one Old Testament.[6] In this Scriptorium,

---

[3] Middle English Dictionary (online): "ars, n"; "intestine, n." Oxford English Dictionary (online): "intestine, n."
[4] "John Wyclif," *Wikipedia*, http://en.wikipedia.org/wiki/John_Wy clif (accessed May 18, 2014). More recently, and in a different sort of popular media, BBC 4's *In Our Time* broadcast a discussion, "John Wyclif and the Lollards," that made the same claims in its introduction: Melvyn Bragg, "John Wyclif and the Lollards," *In Our Time*, BBC 4, June 16, 2011, http://www.bbc.co.uk/programmes/b011vh4k (accessed May 18, 2014).
[5] Ronald Lukens-Bull and Mark Fafard, "Next Year in Orlando: (Re)Creating Israel in Christian Zionism," *Journal of Religion and Society* 9 (2007): http://moses.creighton.edu/JRS/2007/2007-16.html (accessed May 18, 2014). Eric Spitznagel, "Holy Crap: The Unhappiest Place on Earth," *Vanity Fair*, December 17, 2008, http://www. vanityfair.com/online/daily/2008/12/the-unhappiest-place-on-earth. html (accessed May 18, 2014).
[6] See *The Scriptorium: Center for Biblical Antiquities*, http://www.

Wyclif is depicted as hard at work on the translation, alone. When viewing the animatronic Wyclif, "the audience hears the sounds of an angry crowd supposedly just outside the room. Wycliffe then enjoins the audience to take copies of the Bible and leave through the fireplace that swings opens to a secret passageway. The visitor is encouraged to imagine that they are participating in the early efforts of Protestantism."[7] As incorrect as the history depicted here may be, the free circulation of an open, English Bible in the face of powerful institutional efforts to keep it closed and proprietary is represented forcefully. Expressed here is a yearning for an offer to participate in a successful resistance against institutional forces that threaten the bedrocks of culture: religion and language itself. No wonder we wish to put a face on that resistance.

Thanks to complicated networks of control, intellectual piracy is on the rise in the twenty-first century. Perhaps this is part of why we search for a cultural warrior like "Wyclif" regardless of any attachment we may or may not have to Sola Scriptura. As copyrights and patents get increasingly finely-grained one can be a pirate and not even know it. A couple of unexpected examples will illustrate the degree to which control over traditional information commons have been exerted in the twenty-first century. In 2008, animator Nina Paley was beginning to tour her film, *Sita Sings the Blues* on the independent film festival circuit when her project's success was abruptly halted. Despite her careful research into the images and music she had recycled and transformed in the making of her film, she faced a demand to cease for-profit production of *Sita* unless she paid royalties. While the 80-year old music recordings she had chosen were in the public domain, Paley had not discovered in her research that the arrangements

---

holylandexperience.com/exhibits/the_scriptorium.html, and Mary Dove's list of existing Wycliffite Bibles in the appendix of *The First English Bible: The Text and Context of the Wycliffite Versions* (Cambridge, UK: Cambridge University Press, 2007).

[7] Lukens-Bull and Fafard, "Next Year in Orlando," 24.

themselves remained under copyright. The animator's attempts to find a distributor came to nothing and she was suddenly facing a mountain of debt.[8] Paley found that her only recourse was to release the film for free, to give it away under a creative commons license, and to hope that merchandise sales and donations would eventually erase the debt.[9] Examples of media developers being silenced by aggressive copyright policing can be multiplied. An ironic example of this is Lawrence Lessig's tutorials on fair use being removed from YouTube for potential copyright violations in 2008 and 2010.[10] Notably, Lessig fought this action in court and settled in return for compensation and an adjustment of his antagonist's takedown procedure.[11]

Bioengineering is another contentious area of intellectual piracy. Most commercial seed crops (including cotton) developed by the agricultural industry in the US today are patented.[12] Traditional farming practices like saving seeds from

---

[8] Dan Schreiber, "Copyrighting Away Culture: An Interview with Nina Paley," *Smile Politely: Champaign-Urbana's Online Magazine*, April 9, 2009 http://smilepolitely.com/arts/copy-righting_away_cul ture_an_interview_with_nina_paley/ (accessed May 18, 2014).

[9] *Sita Sings the Blues* License: http://www.sitasingstheblues.com/license.html (accessed May 18, 2014).

[10] Mike Masnik, "Bogus Copyright Claim Silences Yet Another Larry Lessig Youtube Presentation," *Techdirt*, March 2, 2010, http://techdirt.com/articles/20100302/0354498358.shtml (accessed May 18, 2014).

[11] "Lawrence Lessig Settles Fair Use Lawsuit Over Phoenix Music Snippets," *Electronic Frontier Foundation*, February 27, 2014, https://www.eff.org/press/releases/lawrence-lessig-settles-fair-use-lawsuit-over-phoenix-music-snippets (accessed May 18, 2014).

[12] "Seed Piracy a Risky Bet," *Farm Industry News*, November 1, 1998, http://farmindustrynews.com/mag/farming_seed_piracy_risky/ (accessed May 18, 2014); Hisane Masaki, "Japan Revs Up Farm Export Drive," *Asia Times Online*, January 18, 2006, http://www.atimes.com/atimes/Japan/HA18Dh03.html (accessed May 18, 2014); Pallab Ghosh, "India's GM Seed Piracy," *BBC News*, June 17, 2003, http://news.bbc.co.uk/2/hi/science/nature/2998150.stm (accessed May 18, 2014); Chris Boning, "Seed Piracy Remains Center of Lawsuits,"

season to season, or perhaps simply planting a field next to a field of genetically engineered crop year after year and letting cross-pollination do its work can lead to charges of piracy when patented seeds are involved.[13] Running an internet search on "seed piracy" turns up as many or more hits by seed companies explaining responsibilities and rights as it does news articles, however, and seed piracy appears to remain a relatively unknown issue except for people in affected areas and industries.[14]

Truman State University Index, April 10, 2008, http://index.truman.edu/pdf/2007-2008/April10/page8.pdf (accessed May 18, 2014). The Supreme Court has ruled recently in support of seed patents: Nina Totenberg, "For Supreme Court, Monsanto's Win Was More About Patents Than Seeds," NPR, May 13, 2013, http://www.npr.org/blogs/thesalt/2013/05/14/183729491/Supreme-Court-Sides-With-Monsanto-In-Seed-Patent-Case (accessed May 18, 2014). In response, a fledgling movement to develop open source seeds has begun: Dan Charles, "Plant Breeders Release First 'Open Source Seeds'," NPR, April 17, 2014, http://www.npr.org/blogs/thesalt/2014/04/17/303772556/plant-breeders-release-first-open-source-seeds (accessed May 18, 2014).

[13] Windblown pollination is a defense used commonly by farmers being sued by seed companies, and can be found frequently in interviews with embattled farmers. For a legal opinion, see Stephanie M. Bernhardt, "High Plains Drifting: Wind-Blown Seeds and the Intellectual Property Implications of the GMO Revolution," *Northwestern Journal of Technology and Intellectual Property* 4 (2005): http://www.law.northwestern.edu/jour-nals/njtip/v4/n1/1/ (accessed May 18, 2014). For a recent discovery of how common cross-pollination is among canola (otherwise known as rapeseed) populations, see Geoffrey Brumfiel, "Genetically Modified Canola 'Escapes' Farm Fields," NPR, August 6, 2010, http://www.npr.org/tem-plates/story/story.php?sto-ryId=129010499 (accessed May 18, 2014).

[14] See for example the striking set of pages developed by seed company Monsanto to educate about the illegality and immorality of seed piracy, "Technology Protection," http://www.monsanto.ca/ourcommitments/Pages/technologyprotection.aspx (accessed May 18, 2014). Among others, also see the infosheet "Seed Piracy Prevention" provided by Great Lakes Hybrids, http://www.greatlakeshybrids.com/technology/seed-piract-prevention (accessed May 18,

The cherry-picked examples of intellectual piracy I employ in this epilogue could be expanded almost without limit, but the pattern to them all remains the same: institutions or corporations claim as property ideas or material members of the public claim to be common based on traditional practices. Effluorescence of intellectual piracy at this moment of political and technological revolution cannot help but draw us to look back and see that the enforcement of intellectual property in the face of traditional information culture has occurred before. In the religious arena these occurrences are celebrated because of faith measurable in acts of martyrdom, but the erupting stratum carries with it more of the traditional information commons than religious works alone. We have seen that despite the radically different stakes involved, in the late Middle Ages, law texts traced the same trajectory as religious texts. In the end, perhaps religious texts serve as cultural bellwethers for the health of the information commons in all areas. As unlikely as it might seem, we might consider seriously the import of an animatronic Wyclif, gesturing us to follow him on a (potentially doomed) quest to preserve the information commons.

2014). For an example of local response see Martha Quillin, "In North Carolina, a 20-fold Increase in Fines for Seed Piracy," *The State*, May 18, 2014, http://www.thestate.com/2014/05/18/3453155/in-north-carolina-a-20-fold-increase.html (accessed May 18, 2014).

References

A. Manuscripts

Alnwick Castle, MS 449
Bel Air, CA, Dr. Steve Somer
Cambridge, MA, Harvard University Library, MS Richardson 3
Cambridge, University Library, MS Additional 2827
Cambridge, University Library, MS Dd 15. 18
Cambridge, University Library, MS Ff. 2. 38
Cambridge, University Library, MS Ii 6. 10
Cambridge, University Library, MS Ii 6. 25
Cambridge, Magdalene College, MS Pepys 2073
Cambridge, St. John's College, MS E. 14
Cambridge, Trinity College Cambridge, MS R. 3. 20
Eton, Eton College, MS 24
Kew, National Archives, MS C/49/2/10
London, British Library, MS Additional 10596
London, British Library, MS Additional 36999
London, British Library, MS Additional 41175
London, British Library, MS Cotton Claudius D. II
London, British Library, MS Egerton 1995

London, British Library, MS Egerton 617
London, British Library, MS Egerton 618
London, British Library, MS Harley 2332
London, British Library, MS Harley 4999
London, British Library, MS Egerton 2880
London, British Library, MS Lansdowne 796
London, British Library, MS Sloane 1313
London, British Library, MS Sloane 1853
London, British Library, MS Stowe 880
London, British Library, MS Royal 17 A. XVI
London, British Library, MS Royal 1 C. VIII
Manchester, John Rylands University Library, MS English 77
Manchester, John Rylands University Library, MS English 81
New York, Columbia University Library, MS Plimpton Additional 3
New York, Morgan Library, MS M. 99
Oxford, Bodleian Libraries, MS Bodley 277
Oxford, Bodleian Libraries, MS Bodley 771
Oxford, Bodleian Libraries, MS Douce 16
Oxford, Bodleian Libraries, MS Douce 27
Oxford, Bodleian Libraries, MS Douce 232
Oxford, Bodleian Libraries, MS Douce 240
Oxford, Bodleian Libraries, MS Douce 265
Oxford, Bodleian Libraries, MS Douce Charters 62 (Douce Charters a. 1. f. 9)
Oxford, Bodleian Libraries, MS Laud Misc. 286
Oxford, Bodleian Libraries, MS Rawlinson B. 520
Oxford, Bodleian Libraries, MS Rawlinson C. 258
Oxford, Bodleian Libraries, MS Rawlinson D. 939
Oxford, Bodleian Libraries, MS Tanner 407
Oxford, Balliol College, MS 354
Oxford, New College, MS 320
San Marino, Huntington Library, MS HM 142
Tokyo, Takamiya collection, MS 219
Wolfenbuttel, Herzog-August-Bibliothek, Cod. Guelf. Aug. A. 2
Worcester, Worcester Cathedral Library, MS F. 172

B. Printed Primary Sources

Baildon, William, ed. *Records of the Honourable Society of Lincoln's Inn*, Vol. 1. London: Lincoln's Inn, 1896.

Bramley, Henry, ed. *The Psalter: Or Psalms of David and Certain Canticles.* Oxford: Clarendon, 1884.

Cooper, W.R. ed. *The New Testament. Translated by William Tyndale. The Text of the Worms Edition of 1526 in the Original Spelling.* London: The British Library, 2000.

Dove, Mary, ed. *The Earliest Advocates of the English Bible: The Texts of the Medieval Debate.* Exeter: University of Exeter Press, 2010.

Edden, Valerie, ed. *Richard Maidstone's Pentitential Psalms edited from Oxford, Bodleian Library, MS Rawlinson A 389.* Heidelburg: Carl Winter, 1990.

Foxe, John. *Acts and Monuments.* London: John Day, 1570.

Franke, M. Friedrich, ed. *D. Martin Luther's* Kirchenpostille. Leipzig: Gebauersche Buchhandlung E. Schimmel, 1846.

Harris, Mary Dormer, ed. *The Coventry Leet Book.* 4 vols. Early English Text Society: London, 1907-13.

Hudson, Anne, ed. *Two Revisions of Richard Rolle's English Psalter Commentary and Related Canticles.* Oxford: Oxford University Press, 2013.

---. *Selections from English Wycliffite Writings.* Cambridge, UK: Cambridge University Press, 1978.

Lloyd, William Forster. *Prices of Corn in Oxford in the Beginning of the Fourteenth Century.* Cambridge, MA: Harvard University Press, 1830.

Macracken, Henry, ed. *The Minor Poems of John Lydgate,* Vol. 1. Oxford: Oxford University Press, 1911.

Reusch, Fr. Heinrich. *Die Indices Librorum Prohibitorum des Sechzehnten Jahrhunderts.* Tübingen: H. Laupp, 1886.

Statutes of the Realm. 11 vols. London: Record Commission, 1810-1825.

Stockton, Eric, ed. *The Major Latin Works of John* Gower. Seattle: University of Washington Press, 1962.

STC 864. *Here begynnethe the boke named the assyse of bread.* [London]: Richard Bankes: [not after 1532].

STC 866. *Here begynneth the boke named the assyse of breade.* [London]: Robert Wyer, [1544?].

STC 867. [*The Assize of Bread.*] [London: Robert Wyer], [1546?].

STC 868.2. *Here begynneth the boke named the assyse of breade.* [London]: Robert Wyer, [1553?].

STC 868.4 *Here begynneth the boke named the Assyse of breade.* [London]: Robert Wyer, [1555?].

STC 868.6. *Here begynneth the boke named the Assise of bread.* [[London]: Thomas Colwell, dwellynge in the house of Robert wyer [1560]].

STC 868.8. *Here begynneth the booke named the assise of bread.* [London: Thomas Colwell, [1570]].

STC 869. *Here beginneth the booke, named the asise of breade.* [London: Hugh Jackson, [ca. 1580]].

STC 869.5. *Here beginneth the booke, named the aßise of breade.* [London: Hugh Jackson, [ca. 1580]].

STC 2063.3. Miles Coverdale. *Biblia the Byble, that is, the holy Scrypture of the Olde and New Testament, faithfully translated in to Englyshe.* [Antwerp: Marten de Keyser, 1535].

STC 2066. John Rogers. *The Byble which Is all the holy Scripture: in whych are contayned the Olde and Newe Testament truly and purely translated into Englysh by Thomas Matthew.* [London: Richard Grafton and Edward Whitchurch, 1537].

STC 2070.1 John Rastell. *Exposicio[n]es t[er]mi[n]o[rum] legu[m] anglo[rum].* London: John Rastell, [1523].

STC 2350. William Tyndale. [The Pentateuch]. [Antwerp: Marten de Keyser, 1530].

STC 2351. William Tyndale. *The first boke of Moses called Genesis newly correctyd and amendyd by W.T.* [Antwerp: Marten de Keyser, 1534].

STC 2777. George Joye. *The prophete Isaye, translated into englysshe, by George Ioye.* [Antwerp: Marten de Keyser, 1531].

STC 2823. William Tyndale. [*The New Testament*]. [Cologne: Peter Quentell?, 1525].

STC 2824. William Tyndale. [*The newe Testame[n]t, as it was written and caused to be writte[n] by them which herde yt*]. [Worms: Peter Schöffer?, 1526?].

STC 2826. William Tyndale. *The newe Testament, dylygently corrected and compared with the Greke by Willyam Tindale.* [Antwerp: Marten de Keyser, 1534].

STC 2827. George Joye. *The hole new Testament with the Pistles taken out of the olde Testament to be red in the chirche.* [Antwerp: Catharyn wydowe [of C. Ruremond], 1535].

STC 9272. *The great boke of statutes* [London: Robert Redman, 1533?].

STC 9275. *The great Charter called i[n] latyn Magna Carta.* [London: Elizabeth Pickering, 1541?].

STC 9276. *The great charter called in latyn Magna Carta.* [London: Thomas Petit, [1542]].

STC 9286. *The boke of Magna Carta.* [London: Robert Redman], 1534.

STC 9515.5. *The statutes prohemium.* [London]: John Rastell, [1519].

STC 9518. *The statutes prohemium.* [[London]: John Rastell, [1527]].

STC 9519. *Here begynnith the hole abrygeme[n]t of al the statut[es].* [London: Robert Redman, [1528]].

STC 9521. *The grete abbregement of the statutys of Englond.* [London?]: William Rastell, [1531?].

STC 9521a.5. [*The grete abbregement of the statutys*]. [London?: Robert Redman, 1533?]

STC 9522. *The greate abbrydgement of all ye statutes of Englande.* [London: Robert Redman,] [1538?].

STC 9523. *The great abredgement of all the statutes of Englande.* [London: Thomas Petit,] [1542].

STC 9525. *The newe greate abredgement brefly conteynynge, all thactes and statutes of this realme of England.* London: Thomas Gaultier, 1551.

STC 9526. *The newe greate abredgement.* [London: William Powell,] 1551.

STC 9618. *De termino Mich[ael]is anno p[ri]mo H. vi.* [[London]: Robert Redman, [1526?]].

STC 9779. *De termi[n]o Pasche An[no] s[e]c[un]do. E. iiij.* [[London]: Richard Pynson, [1510?]].

STC 9780. *De termino Pasche anno secundo. E. iiii.* [London: Robert Redman, 1525?].

STC 9826. *De termino Pasche anno. ix. Edwardi quarti.* [London: Richard Pynson, [1525?]].

STC 9827. *De termino Pasche anno ix Edwardi.iiii.* [London: Robert Redman, [1525?]].

STC 9838.7. *De termino Pashe anno xii E. IIII.* [London]: Robert Redman, [1526?].

STC 9839. *De termino Pasche. Anno .xii. Edwardi.iiii.* [London: Richard Pynson, [1526?]].

STC 9944.5. *De termino Michaelis anno. xiiii. H. viii.* [London]: Robert Redman, [1527?].

STC 9945. *De termino Michaelis anno. xiiii. H. viii.* [London]: Richard Pynson, [1528?].

STC 14820. George Joye. *An apologye made by George Ioye to satisfye (if it maye be) w. Tindale.* [Antwerp, widow of C. Ruremond,] 1535.

STC 15726. Thomas Littleton. *Lyttylton tenures newly and moost truly correctyd [et] amendyd* [London: Richard Pynson, 1525].

STC 15727. Thomas Littleton. *Lytylton tenures newly and most truly correctyd [and] amendyd.* [London: Robert Redman], [1528].

STC 15728. Thomas Littleton. *Lytylton tenures newly and most truly corrected [and] amended.* [London: Richard Pynson], [1528].

STC 15729. Thomas Littleton. *Lytylton tenures newly and most truly corrected [and] amended.* [London: Richard Pynson], [1528].

STC 15730. Thomas Littleton. *Lyttylton tenures newly imprinted.* [London: Robert Redman], [ca. 1530].

STC 15986. *A prymer in Englyshe.* [London: Johan Byddell for Wyllyam Marshall, [1534]].

STC 15986.3. *This prymer of Salysbery vse, bothe ein Englyshe & in Latyn.* [London]: Robert Redman, 1535.

STC 17728. Clement Maidstone. *Ordinale Sarum.* [[London]: Richard Pynson, [1503]].
STC 23879.7. *The Tenuris.* [London: John Rastell, [ca. 1523]].
STC 23880. *Olde teners newly corrected.* [London: Richard Pynson], [1525].
STC 23880.3. *The Tennris.* [London: John Rastell, 1525].
STC 23880.5. *Olde teners newly corrected.* [London: Robert Redman, [1528]].
STC 24440. William Tyndale. *An exposicion vppon the. v. vi. vii. chapters of Mathew.* [Antwerp?: de Keyser, 1533?].
STC 24443. William Tyndale. *The exposition of the fyrste epistle of seynt Jhon with a prologge before it.* [Antwerp: Marten de Keyser], 1531.
STC 24454. William Tyndale. [*Parable of the wicked mammon*]. [Antwerp, 1528].
Wilkins, David, ed. *Concilia Magnae Britanniae et Hiberniae.* 4 vols. London: Gosling, Gyles, Woodward, and Davis, 1737.

C. Printed Secondary Sources

Arblaster, Paul. "Domein de Waghemaker? Front Elevation of the English House." In *Tyndale's Testament*, eds. Paul Arblaster, Gergely Juhász and Guido Latré, 80–81. Turnhout: Brepols, 2002.

Armstrong, Elizabeth. *Before Copyright: The French Book-Privilege System 1498-1526.* Cambridge, UK: Cambridge University Press, 1990.

Avis, Frederick C. "England's Use of Antwerp Printers, 1500-1540." *Gutenberg-Jahrbuch* (1973): 234–240.

Baker, J.H. *Oxford History of the Laws of England.* Vol. 6. Oxford: Oxford University Press, 2003.

Baugh, Albert C. and Thomas Cable. *A History of the English Language.* 5th edn. Upper Saddle River: Prentice Hall, 2002.

Bennett, Judith. *Ale, Beer, and Brewsters in England: Women's Work in a Changing World, 1300-1600.* Oxford: Ox-

ford University Press, 1996.
Bentley, Elna-Jean Young. *The Formulary of Thomas Hoccleve*. Ph.D. diss., Emory University, 1965.
Blagden, Cyprian. *The Stationers' Company: A History, 1403-1959*. Stanford: Stanford University Press, 1960.
Blayney, Peter. *The Stationers' Company before the Charter, 1403-1557*. London: Worshipful Company of Stationers and Newspaper Makers, 2003.
Bradley, Dale A. "The Divergent Anarcho-Utopian Discourses of the Open Source Software Movement." *Canadian Journal of Communication* 30 (2005): 585–611.
Brand, Paul. "The Languages of the Law in Later Medieval England." In *Multilingualism in Later Medieval Britain*, ed. D.A. Trotter, 63–76. Cambridge, UK: D.S. Brewer, 2000).
Braudel, Fernand. *La Méditerranée et le Monde Méditerranéen*. 2nd edn. Paris: Librairie Armand Colin, 1966.
Brodie, D.M. "Edmund Dudley: Minister of Henry VII." *Transactions of the Royal Historical Society* 15 (1932): 133–161.
Butterworth, Charles. *The English Primers (1529-1545): Their Publication and Connection with the English Bible and the Reformation in England*. New York: Octagon Books, 1971.
Butterworth, Charles and Allan Chester. *George Joye 1495?-1553: A Chapter in the History of the English Bible and the English Reformation*. Philadelphia: University of Pennsylvania Press, 1962.
Carey, Hilary M. "What is the Folded Almanac? The Form and Function of a Key Manuscript Source for Astromedical Practice in Later Medieval England." *Society History of Medicine* 16 (2003): 482–509.
---. "Astrological Medicine and the Medieval English Folded Almanac." *Social History of Medicine* 17 (2004): 345–363.
Clanchy, M.T. *From Memory to Written Record: England 1066-1307*. 2nd edn. Oxford: Oxford University Press, 1993.
Clark, James Andrew. "Norm and License in Tyndale's New

Testament Translation." In *William Tyndale and the Law*, eds. John A.R. Dick and Anne Richard, 59–68. Kirksville, MO: Sixteenth Century Journal Publishers, 1994.

Coleman, E. Gabriella. *Coding Freedom: The Ethics and Aesthetics of Hacking*. Princeton: Princeton University Press, 2013.

Coleman, Joyce. *Public Reading and the Reading Public in Late Medieval England and France*. Cambridge, UK: Cambridge University Press, 1996.

Connolly, Margaret. *John Shirley: Book Production and the Noble Household in Fifteenth-Century England*. Aldershot, UK: Ashgate, 1998.

Copeland, Rita. *Rhetoric, Hermeneutics, and Translation in The Middle Ages: Academic Traditions and Vernacular Texts*. Cambridge, UK: Cambridge University Press, 1995.

---. "Toward a Social Genealogy of Translation Theory: Classical Property Law and Lollard Property Reform." In *Translation Theory and Practice in the Middle Ages*, ed. Jeanette Beer, 173–183. Kalamazoo: Medieval Institute Publications, 1997.

---. *Pedagogy, Intellectuals, and Dissent in the Later Middle Ages*. Cambridge, UK: Cambridge University Press, 2001.

Cowley, John D. *A Bibliography of Abridgments, Digests, Dictionaries, and Indexes of English Law to the Year 1800*. London: Quaritch, 1932.

Daniell, David. "Tyndale, Roye, Joye, and Copyright." In *William Tyndale and the Law*, eds. John A.R. Dick and Anne Richardson, 93–101. Kirksville, MO: Sixteenth Century Journal Publishers, 1994.

---. *William Tyndale: A Biography*. New Haven: Yale University Press, 1994.

Davis, James. "Baking for the Common Good: a Reassessment of the Assize of Bread in Medieval England." *Economic History Review* 57 (2004): 465–502.

Deazley, Ronan, Martin Kretschmer and Lionel Bently, eds. *Privilege and Property: Essays on the History of Copyright*. London: OpenBook Publishers, 2010.

Devereux, E.J. *A Bibliography of John Rastell*. Montreal: Mc-

Gill-Queen's University Press, 1999.

DiBona, Chris, Danese Cooper and Mark Stone, eds. *Open Sources 2.0: The Continuing Evolution*. New York: O'Reilly, 2006.

Dove, Mary. *The First English Bible: Text and Context of the Wycliffite Versions*. Cambridge, UK: Cambridge University Press, 2007.

Elton, G.R. *England under the Tudors*. 3rd edn. London: Routledge, 1991.

Erler, Mary C. "Devotional Literature." In *The Cambridge History of the Book in Britain, Vol. 3: 1400-1557*, eds. Lotte Hellinga and J.B. Trapp, 495–525. Cambridge, UK: Cambridge University Press, 1999.

Eisenstein, Elizabeth. *The Printing Press as an Agent of Change: Communications and Cultural Transformations in Early-Modern Europe*, Vols. 1-2. Cambridge, UK: Cambridge University Press, 1979.

Everett, Dorothy. "The Middle English Prose Psalter of Richard Rolle of Hampole." *Modern Language Review* 17 (1922): 217–227.

Fennell, Claire. "The Assize of Bread (1256)." In *Beowulf and Beyond*, eds. Hans Sauer and Renate Bauer, 183–196. Frankfurt am Main: Peter Lang, 2007.

Ferguson, Meraud Grant. "'In Recompense of His Labours and Inuencyon': Early Sixteenth-Century Book Trade Privileges and the Birth of Literary Property in England." *Transactions of the Cambridge Bibligraphical Society* 13 (2004): 14–32.

Fisher, John. "Chancery and the Emergence of Standard Written English in the Fifteenth Century." *Speculum* 52 (1977): 870–899.

Foys, Martin. *Virtually Anglo-Saxon: Old Media, New Media, and Early Medieval Studies in the Late Age of Print*. Gainesville: University Press of Florida, 2007.

Friedman, John B. "Harry the Hayward and Talbot his Dog: An Illustrated Girdlebook from Worcestershire." In *Art into Life: Collected Papers from the Kresge Art Museum Medieval Symposia*, eds. Carol Garrett Fischer and Kathleen L. Scott, 115–153. East Lansing: Michigan State University Press, 1995.

Ghosh, Kantik. *Wycliffite Heresy: Authority and the Interpretation of Texts.* Cambridge, UK: Cambridge University Press, 2002.

Giancarlo, Matthew. *Parliament and Literature in Late Medieval England.* Cambridge, UK: Cambridge University Press, 2007.

Gitelman, Lisa. *Always Already New: Media, History, and the Data of Culture.* Cambridge, MA: M.I.T. Press, 2006.

Gleason, John B. "The Earliest Evidence for Ecclesiastical Censorship of Printed Books in England." *The Library* 4 (1982): 135–141.

Graham, Howard Jay. "The Rastells and the Printed English Law Book of the Renaissance." *Law Library Journal* 7 (1954): 6–25.

---. "'Our Tong Maternall Maruellously Amendyd and Augmentyd': The First Englishing and Printing of the Medieval Statutes at Large, 1530-1533." *UCLA Law Review* 59 (1965-1966): 59–98.

Greene, Jody. *The Trouble with Ownership: Literary Property and Authorial Liability in England, 1660-1730.* Philadelphia: University of Pennsylvania Press, 2005.

Greg, W.W. "*Ad Imprimendum Solum.*" *The Library*, 3rd series, 9 (1954): 242–247.

Gustafson, Kevin. "Richard Rolle's English Psalter and the Making of a Lollard Text." *Viator* 33 (2002): 294–309.

de Hamel, Christopher. "Books of Hours 'Imaging' the Word." In *The Bible as Book: The Manuscript Tradition*, eds. John Sharpe III and Kimberly van Kampen, 137–143. London: British Library, 1998.

---. *The Book: A History of the Bible.* London: Phaidon Press, 2001.

Hanna, Ralph. *London Literature, 1300-1380.* Cambridge, UK: Cambridge University Press, 2005.

Hardt, Michael and Antonio Negri. *Commonwealth.* Cambridge, MA: The Belknap Press, 2009.

Herman, Peter. "John Rastell *(London: 1509?- 1536?)* William

Rastell London: (1539-1534)." In *The British Literary Book Trade, 1475-1700*, eds. James Bracken and Joel Silver, 213. Washington, DC: Gale, 1996.

Himanen, Pekka. *The Hacker Ethic*. New York: Random House, 2001.

Hobbins, Daniel. *Authorship and Publicity before Print: Jean Gerson and the Transformation of Late Medieval Learning*. Philadelphia: University of Pennsylvania Press, 2009.

Hobbs, Gerald. "Martin Bucer and the Englishing of the Psalms: Pseudonymity in the Service of Early English Protestant Piety." In *Martin Bucer: Reforming Church and Community*, ed. D.F. Wright, 161–175. Cambridge, UK: Cambridge University Press, 1994.

Den Hollander, A.A. *De Nederlandse Bijbel Vertalingen 1522-1545*. Niewkoop: De Graaf Publishers, 1997.

Hope, Andrew. "Ban on Possession of English New Testaments, Antwerp 1527." In *Tyndale's Testament*, eds. Paul Arblaster, Gergely Juhász and Guido Latré, 151–152. Turnhout: Brepols, 2002.

---. "On the Smuggling of Prohibited Books from Antwerp to England in the 1520s and 1530s." In *Tyndale's Testament*, eds. Paul Arblaster, Gergely Juhász and Guido Latré, 35–38. Turnhout: Brepols, 2002.

---. "Plagiarizing the Word of God: Tyndale between More and Joye." In *Plagiarism in Early Modern England*, ed. Paulina Kewes, 93–105. New York: Palgrave, 2003.

Horowitz, Mark. "'Agree with the king': Henry VII, Edmund Dudley, and the Strange Case of Thomas Sunnyff." *Historical Research* 79 (2006): 325–366.

---. "Policy and Prosecution in the Reign of Henry VII." *Historical Research* 82 (2009): 412–458.

Hudson, Anne. "Wyclif and the English Language." In *Wyclif in His Times*, ed. Anthony Kenny, 85–103. Oxford: Clarendon, 1986.

Huhtamo, Erkki. "From Kaleidoscomaniac to Cybernerd: Notes Toward an Archeology of Media." In *Electronic Culture: Technology and Visual Representation*, ed. Timothy Druckrey, 296–302. New York: Aperture, 1996.

Johns, Adrian. *Piracy: Intellectual Property Wars from Gutenberg to Gates*. Chicago: University of Chicago Press, 2009.

Johnston, Andrew G. "L'imprimerie et la Réforme aux Pays-Bas, 1520-c.1555." In *La Réforme et le Livre*, eds. Andrew G. Johnston and Jean-François Gilmont, 155–185. Paris: Cerf, 1990.

Johnston, Andrew G. and and Jean-François Gilmont. "L'imprimerie et la Réforme à Anvers." In *La Réforme et le Livre*, eds. Andrew G. Johnston and Jean-François Gilmont, 191–216. Paris: Cerf, 1990.

Jushász, Gergely. "The Bible and the Early Reformation Period." In *Tyndale's Testament,* eds. Paul Arblaster, Gergely Juhász and Guido Latré, 27. Turnhout: Brepols, 2002.

---. "George Joye, An *Apologye Made By George Joye, to Satisfy, If It May Be, W. Tindale*, 1535, edited by Edward Arber (The English Scholar's Library 13; Birmingham, 1882)." In *Tyndale's Testament*, eds. Paul Arblaster, Gergely Juhász and Guido Latré, 161. Turnhout: Brepols, 2002.

---. "Some Neglected Aspects of the Exegetical Debate on Resurrection and the Immortality of the Soul between William Tyndale and George Joye in Antwerp (1534-1535)." *Reformation* 14 (2009): 1–47.

---. Gergely M. Jushász. *Translating Resurrection: An Early Sixteenth-Century Exegetical Debate in Antwerp Between the Protestant Bible Translators William Tyndale and George Joye and its Historical and Theological Context*. Ph.D. diss., Katholieke Universiteit Leuven, 2008.

---. *Translating Resurrection: the Debate Between William Tyndale and George Joye and Its Historical and Theological Context*. Leiden: Brill, 2014.

Kelly, Henry Ansgar. *Inquisitions and Other Trial Procedures in the Medieval West*. Aldershot, UK: Ashgate, 2001.

Kennedy, Kathleen E. *The Courtly and Commercial Art of the Wycliffite Bible*. Turnhout: Brepols, 2014.

---. "Prosopography of the Book and the Politics of Legal Language in Late Medieval England." *Journal of British*

Studies 53 (2014): 565–587.

---. "Reintroducing the English Books of Hours, or 'English Primers.'" *Speculum* 89 (2014): 693–723.

---. "A London Legal Miscellany, Popular Law, and Medieval Print Culture." In *Truth and Tales: Cultural Mobility and Medieval Media*, eds. Nicholas Watson and Fiona Somerset. Columbus: Ohio State University Press, 2015 (forthcoming).

Kim, Eugene. "Everything is Known." In *Open Sources 2.0: The Continuing Evolution*, eds. Chris DiBona, Danese Cooper and Mark Stone, 297–306. New York: O'Reilly, 2006.

King, John. "'The Light of Printing,' William Tyndale, John Foxe, John Day, and Early Modern Print Culture." *Renaissance Quarterly* 54 (2001): 52–85.

Kreps, Barbara. "Elizabeth Pickering: the First Woman to Print Law Books in England and the Relations Within the Community of Tudor London's Printer and Lawyers." *Renaissance Quarterly* 56 (2003): 1053–1088.

Kuczynski, Michael. "Rolle Among the Reformers: Orthodoxy and Heterodoxy in Wycliffite Copies of Richard Rolle's *English Psalter*." In *Mysticism and Spirituality in Medieval England*, eds. William Pollard and Robert Boenig, 177–202. Cambridge, UK: Boydell and Brewer, 1997).

---. *Prophetic Song: The Psalms as Moral Discourse in Late Medieval England*. Philadelphia: University of Pennsylvania Press, 1995.

Kuskin, William. "'Onely Imagined' Vernacular Community and the English Press." In *Caxton's Trace: Studies in the History of English Printing*, ed. William Kuskin, 199–240. Notre Dame: University of Notre Dame Press, 2006.

Latré, Guido. "The 1535 Coverdale Bible and Its Antwerp Origins." In *The Bible as Book: The Reformation*, ed. Orlaith O'Sullivan, 89–102. London: The British Library, 2000.

---. "*Biblia. The bible,* Translated by William Tyndale and Miles Coverdale, edited by Miles Coverdale (n.p., [Antwerp, Merten de Keyser?], 1535)." In *Tyndale's Testa-*

ment, eds. Paul Arblaster, Gergely Juhász and Guido Latré, 143–145. Turnhout: Brepols, 2002.

---. *"The Newe Testament As It Was Written and Caused to Be Written, by Them Which Herde Yt,* [tr. William Tyndale], ([Worms, Peter Schoeffer], [1526])." In *Tyndale's Testament*, eds. Paul Arblaster, Gergely Juhász and Guido Latré, 148–149. Turnhout: Brepols, 2002.

Latrive, Laurent. *Du bon usage de la piraterie*. Paris: Exils, 2004.

Lawton, David. "Dullness and the Fifteenth Century." *ELH* 54 (1987): 761–799.

---. "Englishing the Bible, 1066-1549." In *The Cambridge History of Medieval English Literature*, ed. David Wallace, 454–482. Cambridge, UK: Cambridge University Press, 1999.

Lee, James. "Urban Recorders and the Crown in Late Medieval England." In *The Fifteenth Century, Vol. 3: Authority and Subversion*, ed. Linda Clark, 163–178. Woodbridge, UK: Boydell & Brewer, 2003.

L'Engle, Susan and Robert Gibbs. *Illuminating the Law: Legal Manuscripts in Cambridge Collections*. Turnhout: Harvey Miller, 2001.

Lerer, Seth. *Chaucer and His Readers: Imagining the Author in Late-Medieval England*. Princeton: Princeton University Press, 1993.

Leroquais, Victor. *Les livres d'heures manuscrits de la Bibliothèque Nationale de Paris*. Paris: Protat, 1927.

Lessig, Lawrence. *The Future of Ideas: The Fate of the Commons in a Connected World*. New York: Random House, 2001.

---. *Free Culture: How Big Media Uses Technology and the Law to Lock Down Culture and Control Creativity*. New York: Penguin, 2004.

Levy, Steven. *Hackers: Heroes of the Computer Revolution*. New York: O'Reilly, 2010.

Lewis, Robert E. and Angus McIntosh. *A Descriptive Guide to the Manuscripts of the Prick of Conscience*. Oxford: Society for the Study of Mediaeval Languages and Literature,

1982.

Loades, D.M. "The Press Under the Early Tudors: A Study in Censorship and Sedition." *Transactions of the Cambridge Bibliographical Society* 4 (1968): 29–50.

Loewenstein, Joseph. *The Author's Due: Printing and the Prehistory of Copyright*. Chicago: University of Chicago Press, 2002.

Lovink, Geert. *My First Recession: Critical Internet Culture in Transition*. New York: V2 Publishing, 2003.

Machan, Tim William. "French, English, and the Late Medieval Linguistic Repertoire." In *Language and Culture in Medieval Britain: The French of England c. 1100-c. 1500*, eds. Jocelyn Wogan-Browne, with Carolyn Collette, Maryanne Kowaleski, Linne Mooney, Ad Putter and David Trotter, 363–372. York, UK: University of York Press, 2009.

Mackie, Erin. "Welcome the Outlaw: Pirates, Maroons, and Caribbean Countercultures." *Cultural Critique* 59 (2005): 24–62.

Madero, Marta. *Tabula Picta: Painting and Writing in Medieval Law*, trans. Monique Dascha Inciarte and Roland David Valayre. Philadelphia: University of Pennsylvania Press, 2009.

Matheson, Lister. *The Prose Brut: the Development of a Middle English Chronicle*. Tempe: Medieval and Renaissance Texts and Studies, 1998.

McGlynn, Margaret. "'Of Good Name and Fame in the Countrey,' Standards of Conduct in Henry VII's Chamber Officials." *Historical Research* 82 (2009): 547–559.

McKitterick, David. *Print, Manuscript, and the Search for Order, 1450-1830*. Cambridge, UK: Cambridge University Press, 2003.

Millett, Bella. "Ancrene Wisse and the Book of Hours." In *Writing Religious Women: Female Spirituality and Textual Practices in Late Medieval England*, eds. Denis Renevey and Christiana Whitehead, 21–40. Toronto: University of Toronto Press, 2000.

Nesbitt, Charles. "Mercenary Motives in the Production of

the English Bible in the Early Sixteenth Century." *Anglican Theological Review* 34 (1952): 154–166.

Nissenbaum, Helen. "Hackers and the Contested Ontology of Cyberspace." *New Media and Society* 6 (2004): 195–217.

von Nolcken, Christina. "Lay Literacy, the Democratization of God's Law and the Lollards." In *The Bible as Book: The Manuscript Tradition*, eds. John Sharpe and Kimberly van Kampen, 177–195. London: British Library, 1998.

Oberman, Heiko. *Luther: Man between God and the Devil*. New Haven: Yale University Press, 2006.

O'Reilly, Tim. "The Open Source Paradigm Shift." In *Open Sources 2.0: The Continuing Evolution*, eds. Chris DiBona, Danese Cooper and Mark Stone, 253–272. New York: O'Reilly, 2006.

Ormrod, Mark. "The Use of English: Language, Law, and Political Culture in Fourteenth-Century England." *Speculum* 78 (2003): 750–787.

O'Sullivan, Orlaith. "The Bible Translations of George Joye." In *The Bible as Book: The Reformation*, ed. Orlaith O'Sullivan, 25–38. London: The British Library, 2000.

Peck, Russell. *Kingship and Common Profit in Gower's* Confessio Amantis. Carbondale: Southern Illinois University Press, 1978.

Peikola, Matti. "'First is writen a clause of the bigynnynge therof': The Table of Lections in the Manuscripts of the Wycliffite Bible." *Boletin Millares Carlo* 24-25 (2005-2006): 343–378.

---. "Aspects of *Mise-en-page* in Manuscripts of The Wycliffite Bible." In *Medieval Texts in Context*, eds. Graham Cane and Denise Renevy, 28–67. New York: Routledge, 2008.

Pollard, A.W. "The Regulation of the Book Trade in the Sixteenth Century." *The Library*, 3rd series, 7 (1916): 18–43.

Raymond, Eric S. *The New Hacker's Dictionary*. 3rd edn. Cambridge, MA: M.I.T. Press, 1996.

---. *The Cathedral and the Bazaar: Musings on Linux and Open Source by an Accidental Revolutionary*. New York: O'Reilly, 1999.

Rice, Nicole. *Lay Piety and Religious Discipline in Middle English Literature*. Cambridge, UK: Cambridge University Press, 2008.

Richardson, H.G. and George Sayles. "The Early Statutes." *Law Quarterly Review* 50 (1934): 201–223, 540–571.

Richardson, W.C. *Tudor Chamber Administration, 1485-1547*. Baton Rouge: Louisiana State University Press, 1952.

Robertson, Kellie. *The Laborer's Two Bodies: Labor and the "Work" of the Text in Medieval Britain, 1350-1500*. New York: Palgrave, 2006.

Robinson, P.R. "'Lewdecalendars' from Lynn." In *Tributes to Kathleen L. Scott: English Medieval Manuscripts: Readers, Makers, and Illuminators*, ed. Marlene Villaloboss Hennessy, 221–230. Turnhout: Harvey Miller, 2009.

Rose, Carol. "The Comedy of the Commons: Custom, Commerce, and Inherently Public Property." *University of Chicago Law Review* 53 (1986): 711–781.

Rose, Mark. *Authors and Owners: The Invention of Copyright*. Cambridge, MA: Harvard University Press, 1993.

Ross, Richard. "The Commoning of the Common Law: The Renaissance Debate Over Printing English Law." *University of Pennsylvania Law Review* 146 (1998): 323–461.

Rouse, Richard and Mary Rouse. *Authentic Witnesses: Approaches to Medieval Texts and Manuscripts*. Notre Dame: University of Notre Dame Press, 1991.

Scattergood, V.J. *Politics and Poetry in the Fifteenth Century*. New York: Barnes and Noble, 1972.

Scott, Kathleen L. *Later Gothic Manuscripts, 1390-1490*. 2 vols. New York: Harvey Miller, 1996.

Seabourne, Gwen. "Assize Matters: Regulation of the Price of Bread in Medieval London." *The Journal of Legal History* 27 (2006): 29–52.

Shuger, Debora. *Censorship and Cultural Sensibility: The Regulation of Language in Tudor-Stuart England*. Philadelphia: University of Pennsylvania Press, 2006.

Simpson, James. "Sixteenth-Century Fundamentalism and the Specter of Ambiguity, Or the Literal Sense is Always a

Fiction." In *Writing Fundamentalism*, eds. Axel Stähler and Klaus Stierstorfer, 133–154. Cambridge, UK: Cambridge Scholars, 2009.

---. *Burning to Read: English Fundamentalism and Its Reformation Opponents*. Cambridge, MA: Belknap Press, 2010.

Skemer, Don C. "From Archives to the Book Trade: Private Statute Rolls in England, 1285-1307." *Journal of the Society of Archivists* 16 (1995): 193–206.

---. "Sir William Breton's Book: Production of *Statuta Angliae* in the Late Thirteenth Century." In *English Manuscript Studies, 1100-1700*, eds. Peter Beal and Jeremy Griffiths, 24–51. London: British Library, 1997.

---. "Reading the Law: Statute Books and the Private Transmission of Knowledge in Late Medieval England." In *Learning the Law: Teaching and the Transmission of Law in England, 1150-1900*, eds. Jonathan A. Bush and Alain Wijffels, 115–131. London: British Library, 1999.

Solopova, Elizabeth. "Manuscript Evidence for the Patronage, Ownership and Use of the Wycliffite Bible." In *Form and Function in the Late Medieval Bible*, eds. Eyal Poleg and Laura Light, 333–349. Leiden: Brill, 2013.

Staley, Lynn. "The Penitential Psalms: Conversion and the Limits of Lordship." *Journal of Medieval and Early Modern Studies* 37 (2007): 221–269.

Stallman, Richard. "The GNU Operating System and the Free Software Movement." In *OpenSources: Voices from the Open Source Revolution*, eds. Chris DiBona, Sam Ockman and Mark Stone, 53–70. New York: O'Reilly, 1999.

Tournoy, Gilbert. "*Testamentum Novum* (Basel, Johann Froben, July 1522)." In *Tyndale's Testament*, eds. Paul Arblaster, Gergely Juhász and Guido Latré, 88–89. Turnhout: Brepols, 2002.

Valkema-Blouw, Paul. "Early Modern Protestant Publications in Antwerp, 1526-30: The Pseudonymous Adam Anonymous and Hans Luft of Marlborow." *Quaerendo* 26 (1996): 94–110.

Verheyden, Prosper. "Drukkersoctrooien in de 16e Eeuw." *Tijdschrift voor Boek-en Bibliotheekswezen* 8 (1910): 202–

278.

Wall, Larry. "Diligence, Patience, and Humility." In *Open-Sources: Voices from the Open Source Revolution*, eds. Chris DiBona, Sam Ockman and Mark Stone, 127–148. New York: O'Reilly, 1999.

Warner, Lawrence. *The Lost History of* Piers Plowman: *The Earliest Transmission of Langland's Work*. Philadelphia: University of Pennsylvania Press, 2011.

Watson, Nicholas. *Richard Rolle and The Invention of Authority*. Cambridge, UK: Cambridge University Press, 1991.

Weber, Steven. *The Success of Open Source*. Cambridge, MA: Harvard University Press, 2004.

Westbrook, Vivienne. *Long Travail and Great Paynes: A Politics of Reformation Revision*. Dordrecht: Kluwer Academic Publishers, 2001.

Wieck, Roger S. "The Book of Hours." In *The Liturgy of the Medieval Church*, eds. Thomas J. Heffernan and E. Ann Matter, 473–513. Kalamazoo: Medieval Institute Publications, 2001.

Wogan-Browne, Jocelyn, ed. *Language and Culture in England: The French of England, c. 1100-1500*. York: York Medieval Press, 2009.

Woodbine, George. "The Languages of English Law." *Speculum* 18 (1943): 395–436.

Zielinski, Siegfried. *Deep Time of the Media: Toward and Archaeology of Hearing and Seeing by Technical Means*, trans. Gloria Custance. Cambridge, MA: M.I.T. Press, 2006.

www.ingramcontent.com/pod-product-compliance
Lightning Source LLC
Chambersburg PA
CBHW072045160426
43197CB00014B/2641